AstroGraphology

The hidden link
between your horoscope
and your handwriting

Darrelyn Gunzburg

The Wessex Astrologer

Published in 2009 by
The Wessex Astrologer Ltd
4A Woodside Road
Bournemouth
BH5 2AZ
England

www.wessexastrologer.com

ISBN 9781902405339
A catalogue record of this book is available at The British Library

Cover design by Dave at Creative Byte, Poole, Dorset

Printed and bound in the UK by Cambrian Printers, Aberystwyth

All charts used and astrological calculations generated using Solar Fire Gold.

All Time Maps and artwork designed and laid out by Darrelyn Gunzburg.

Acknowledgements

In the early years of my astrological practice clients would post me a monetary deposit before their consultation. As I opened each client's envelope and read their handwritten note, I began to realize what a gift I held in my hands. A natal chart will display a number of themes and issues, yet none of us works on our whole chart at once, therefore the lines of handwriting in front of me were a living illustration of certain parts of my clients' charts. I recognized that if I could correlate the two systems of handwriting and chart reading, I would better understand which parts of my clients' charts were speaking to me, perhaps those that were most relevant for the coming consultation. Furthermore, since the *Sefer Yetzirah* suggests that meditating on a letter and its shape has a profound effect on how one reaches Wisdom, by changing their letter shapes with focused intention and purpose, my clients could begin to change their narrative and literally rewrite their futures:

> He engraved them, He carved them,
> He permuted them, He weighed them,
> He transformed them,
> And with them, He depicted all that was formed
>   and all that would ever be formed.
>   Kaplan, *Sefer Yetzirah, the Book of Creation,* Revised Edition, p.100.

I set about mapping handwriting to astrology. This book is the result, designed to correlate the two systems of understanding so that you recognize how the underlying patterns within both reflect each other.

To this end I am indebted to all my students who so generously allowed me to work with their handwriting and their charts over the years as I deepened my understanding of this subject. Michael Lutin's ongoing support for the book, and his imprimatur of the title that day at the beach in New York in June 2008, assisted its journey into becoming. Ysha de Donna gave generously of her time and attention as the first-run editor of the manuscript. For her continued support and encouragement I thank Liz Greene. I extend my profound appreciation to Margaret Cahill for her patience and her passion, the two traits of a great editor. As always, the first friend of this work was my life partner, Bernadette Brady, whose relentless enthusiasm, and willingness to explore these ideas with me over the years, allowed this work to emerge. For the extraordinary grace of her presence in my life I give thanks.

Disclaimer

I have been collecting handwriting from many different sources for many years and a large number of examples do not have authors. Any resemblance to an individual's handwriting may simply be that.

Where I have used examples of handwriting from personal communications, then I have obtained permission from the writers to use them. I have not obtained permission to use many of the small phrases, single words and thumbnail layouts. While being true to my commitment in the writing of this book to be clear about the characteristics they reveal, I have in each case endeavoured to be respectful of privacy and dignity.

To the memory of my parents

who gave me my Jewish ancestry

which provided the philosophical roots of this book

Contents

The Empty Page

Before you begin reading this book, buy yourself a notebook in which to write. Write anything, your thoughts, your joys, your wish list, your observations of what is around you. This will give you an anchor for understanding where you are at now with your handwriting and an unbiased place in which to observe and create your letters as you travel the journey of this book.

Introduction

We all put pen to paper. In spite of everything, at the end of the day, in this word-processed, image-rich world, a world of text messages, mobile phones and Skype chats, when we want to jot down a quick thought, we still write with a pen. Granted, personal computers have not only given us the ability to change thought and expression at the press of a key but as email, webcams, internet phone calls, instant messaging, facebooks and virtual realities become the norm, so we use pen and ink less and less to stay in contact with others.

However, have you noticed how many different sorts of pens there are in your stationery shop? The pen section is bigger, slicker, brighter, more colourful than ever before, containing options from gel to biro to ink to fountain pen. Back in 700 CE it was the flight feather of a large bird, preferably a swan, that was all the rage. The finest were taken from the left wing, the ones that curved away from you when you wrote right-handed. Later came the metal dip pen, the fountain pen, and eventually the ball point pen.

Yes, it is true that the task of handwriting has changed greatly as a public function, yet even those who protest that they 'never handwrite nowadays' still use it in some way in their daily lives. An acupuncturist recently confessed to me that he handwrites his case studies for his clients; a database designer told me that he clarifies his thinking by handwriting mindmaps. We scrawl notes to ourselves, many still maintain paper diaries and some of us keep private journals. We scribble quick reminders on Post-It notes. We handwrite cheques. We jot down shopping lists. A few public examinations still require hand-written legible answers. We send Christmas cards, Passover cards, Easter cards, as well as cards at births, deaths and marriages. The most enduring statement we can make to someone at times of deep moment, intimacy and compassion is to send them letters or notes written in our hand. Why this is so and what this means forms part of the subject of this book.

One reason that handwriting endures is that, whilst the computer-written letter ensures legibility, for ease of documentation or the personal touch nothing surpasses the five fingers at the end of our arm. We carry them with us everywhere, connected to our brain and our heart, our emotions and our intellect. Their output reflects our moods, our thoughts and our ability to converse. Most importantly, in the process of creating the letters, we add a piece of our energy to our handwriting through the emotions we feel as we write. If you have ever loved a great masterpiece of art in reproduction and then stood in front of the original in an art gallery, you will understand why. We respond to the energy of a great piece of art because a part of the artist's energy is contained in the paint, the brush strokes, and the canvas or wood that he or she touched. So it is with handwriting. When we receive the personal art we call handwriting from someone we love, we touch and are touched by the real thing.

We take handwriting for granted, yet most of us notice how it changes with different moods, how we prefer to write with a certain pen and in a particular colour, and even the type of paper that feels most comfortable as we write. Most of us have at one time or another, consciously or unconsciously, changed a handwriting trait because it felt better in some way. Most of us have heard about graphology, the study of handwriting to assess somebody's personality from patterns or features of his or her writing.

The word 'graphology' was coined in 1871 by French abbot Jean-Hippolyte Michon. However, graphology has much deeper roots. Nearly 4,000 years ago, around the time of the Code of Hammurabi (c.1792 –1750 BCE) and when Babylon took over from Thebes as the largest city in the world (1770 BCE), the potency of the alphabet and the power of handwriting as magical and divine was contained in an oral code known as the *Sefer Yetzirah*. In this, the earliest document we have about the way letters of the alphabet are shaped and formed, is a set of instructions on how to co-create one's life by following 'thirty-two mystical paths of Wisdom'.[1] This word 'path' was not the commonly used term for a public pathway — 'derekh' — but the word 'netivot' (plural) meaning hidden paths without markers or signposts. Nevertheless the document suggested ways in which these paths may be revealed. According to the *Sefer Yetzirah*, space, the physical universe, is influenced through the physical shape of the letters, time is influenced through meditating on the form of the letters and the spiritual realm is influenced through the sounds of the letters or their names.[2] What links these paths of wisdom with understanding are the letters of the alphabet and the ways they are combined.

---

1. Aryeh Kaplan, *Sefer Yetzirah, the Book of Creation, Revised Edition* (San Francisco: Red Wheel/Weiser, 1997), p.5.
2. Ibid., pp.19-21.

Each letter, says the *Sefer Yetzirah*, represents a different type of information and from their combinations everything is created.

There are at least three known instances in ancient history where the hand of the divine writes. These are the Tablet of Destinies,[3] the Ten Commandments, and 'The writing on the wall' (Daniel 5:5).[4] Writing the words down is the act that makes them true. It is this same writing down of letters that is the focus of this book. In connecting handwriting to a process that uses awareness and focus of intention to create something new, either to reshape a part of the natal chart, or to link it with predictive work, one then co-creates, works together with, the horoscope. This is how I am defining the term 'co-creation'. More than just changing habits, it is an active process of focused attention and persistent presence, watching what arises as one makes the changes and then acting upon that to bring into being a more fulfilling behaviour pattern. So whilst it is a conscious decision made only by you and carried out alone, it is formulated in concert with your natal chart and your predictive work.

We could say that the act of handwriting and the way one shapes and makes letters becomes a personalised model of the *Sefer Yetzirah*, the private expression of the principle articulated in the act of writing the Tablet of Destinies and the Ten Commandments. Since the *Sefer Yetzirah* tells us that the combination of letters expresses the deep human processes of the mind and the soul and carries its manifestation into the outer world, we can take this a step further and recognize that, as a magical entity, the letters have what Bruno Latour calls 'agency', the ability of the letters themselves to take focus and engineer events.[5] As we write the letters on the page we are in a sense, via the *Sefer Yetzirah* and Latour, articulating our world.

The *Sefer Yetzirah* travelled down in time through the oral tradition and was eventually incorporated into a book in Talmudical times (70-500 CE) and used by the Rabbinic sages.[6] In the Gaonic period (6th-10th centuries), Kabbalistic teachers so valued the quality of secrecy that to prevent the information falling

---

3. In Mesopotamian mythology the Tablet of Destinies was envisaged as a clay tablet inscribed with cuneiform writing, also impressed with cylinder seals, which, as a permanent legal document, conferred by divine decree upon the god Enlil his supreme authority as ruler of the universe.

4. *Mene, Mene, Tekel u-Pharsin*: 'Suddenly the fingers of a human hand appeared, and began to write on the plaster of the palace wall, directly behind the lampstand; and the king could see the hand as it wrote.' Jones, Alexander (ed). *The Jerusalem Bible*, Reader's Edition, (Garden City, New York: Doubleday & Company, Inc. 1968), p.1241.

5. Bruno Latour, *We Have Never Been Modern*, trans. Catherine Porter (Cambridge, Massachusetts: Harvard University Press, 1993).

6. Kaplan, *Sefer Yetzirah, the Book of Creation,* Revised Edition, pp. xiv-xv.

into improper hands, they restricted its teachings to small covert societies. In 1562 the first Mantua edition was published,[7] and perhaps due to the stress on silence surrounding the work, the full implications of the power of language and letters at this esoteric level was missed. So when interest in handwriting surfaced in Italy in the form of Alderisius Prosper's book *Ideographia*, published in Bologna in the early seventeenth century, it emerged without conscious knowledge of the *Sefer Yetzirah*, in the wake of the Renaissance interest in the self as centre of the world and shortly before the mechanistic thinking of the Enlightenment. Prosper's book was a systematic attempt to describe the relationship between handwriting and the personality of the hand that wrote it. However, the wisdom of linking shape and magic to handwriting was lost.

This was followed in 1622 by the work of Italian physician Camillo Baldi (1547-1634), in an essay entitled *Trattato Come De Una Lettera Missiva Si Conoscano La Natura E Qualità Dello Scrittore* (Treatise of how, from a formal letter, one can know the nature and quality of the writer) published when he was seventy. Baldi was a Doctor of Medicine and Philosophy, as well as a Professor of Theoretical Medicine, and he taught at the Studio Publico di Bologna for sixty years. Today he is accepted as the father of graphology, even though it was to take another two hundred and forty nine years before the term 'graphology' was coined.

Around 1830 a group of French clerics, including Cardinal Regneir, Archbishop of Cambrai, Bishop Soudinet of Amiens, and Abbé Flandrin, formed a consortium for the serious study of the relationship between handwriting and character using single letter forms as the main source of their information. In 1871 Flandrin's student Abbé Jean-Hippolyte Michon (1806-81) combined the words *grapho* (I write) with *logos* (word, thought, principle, or speech). For over thirty years Michon collected thousands of examples of handwriting and signatures and studied them in minute detail, naming each single element a 'sign' and finding its correspondence in a character trait of the writer. His seven categories included dimension, form, pressure, speed, direction, layout, and continuity. In 1871 Michon founded the Société Francais de Graphologie (SFDG) in Paris, and in the same decade he produced two books *Les Mystères de l'Ecriture* and *La Méthode Practique de Graphologie*,[8] as well publishing *La Graphologie*, which survives today as the quarterly journal of the SFDG.

A few years after Michon's death, his pupil and successor Jules Crépieux-Jamin (1858-1940), whose book *L'ABC de la Graphologie*[9] consolidated fifty years of

---

7. Mantua is a city of northern Italy south-southwest of Verona.
8. Jean-Hippolyte Michon, *Les Mystères De L'écriture; Art De Juger Les Hommes Sur Leurs Autographes* (Paris: 1872) and *Méthode Pratique De Graphologie. L'art De Connaître Les Hommes D'après Leur Écriture* (Paris: Payot, 1878).
9. Jules Crépieux-Jamin, *ABC de la Graphologie*, 2 vols. (Paris: Alcan, 1929).

research, revised the whole of his teacher's work, reclassified and regrouped the signs, and attributed a range of possible meanings to them, declaring that no one single feature in handwriting can reliably represent anything about the writer unless it is supported by other factors in the writing. This theory is still in use and has been taken as the foundation for all professional graphologists. It means that today the best books on graphology acknowledge that, whilst there are many ways of considering the parts, it is how they link together that gives the more complete picture, just as in reading a natal chart.

Nevertheless there is a great chasm between the magical, mystical use of written letters of the *Sefer Yetzirah*, and the concept of the 'science of graphology' as a hierarchical structure of formation and correct headings. Locking the person into a 'type', the alphabet had stranded itself in a sterile land where letters took on form for form's sake. This trend reached a mechanistic high with the graphological psychogram, a system of handwriting analysis developed in 1955 by Klara G. Roman, where a checklist of forty factors, such as balance, harmony, consistency, spacing, and slant, are scored from 0 to 10 and then evaluated.[10] Since the early 1980s more and more graphologists, such as Vimala Rodgers,[11] have taken the approach that changing a stroke in your handwriting can have a profound effect in changing your life, an echo back, consciously or unconsciously, to the *Sefer Yetzirah*.

The final step in this process is what we bring to it as astrologers. The gift of astrology is to give us insights into behaviour and, in my opinion, an ability to predict the shape of the future, not necessarily its outcome. The natal chart is a blueprint full of potentials within certain guidelines, and handwriting via the *Sefer Yetzirah* is the soul engaging with the world. The marriage of the two greatly enriches the astrology. I have termed this process AstroGraphology.

This is a book of change. You are in charge. The *Sefer Yetzirah* points out that the paths to your own understanding are 'netivot', hidden paths without markers or signposts. Each time you pick up a pen you will discover these 'netivot' written in your own hand, drawing from all the light and dark areas of your natal chart. As you understand how your handwriting reflects your natal chart, so you can harness the energy by changing the way you write, helping a difficult aspect to gain a more constructive expression. You can also reshape the landscape that opens up ahead of you via your predictive work, literally creating a different future through your handwriting.

Look carefully at what you find for, as an astrologer, you now have a tool for writing the changes you wish to make on the pages of your life.

---

10. Ruth Gardner, *The Truth About Graphology* (Woodbury: Llewelyn Worldwide, 1991).
11. Vimala Rodgers, *Change Your Handwriting, Change Your Life* (Berkeley: Celestial Arts, 1993).

1

The Rolling Cylinder of Chrysippus

> But surpassing all stupendous inventions, what sublimity of mind was his who dreamed of finding means to communicate his deepest thoughts to any other person, though distant by might intervals of place and time!... and with what facility, by the different arrangements of twenty characters upon a page![1]
>
> Galileo Galilei (1564-1642)

We often complain about our own charts and joke about how we would like to swap it for another but would you really want to do so?

Try this exercise. Look at these handwriting samples (below). First get a quick sense of them without any rationale to back up what you sense. Then select one of them and, on a separate piece of paper, copy it, shape for shape, letter for letter, word for word, line for line, being aware of how you feel and what is happening in your body and your mind. By copying the letters you are stepping into the world of the person who created that handwriting and adopting their basic assumptions of life.

Thank you again so much and we shall be thinking of you all on the 25th...
your sincerely Elizabeth R

---

1. Galilei, Galileo. *Dialogue Concerning the Two Chief World Systems, Ptolemaic and Copernican.* Original edition, 1632, trans. Stillman Drake. Edited by S. J. Gould (New York: The Modern Library, 2001), pp.120-121.

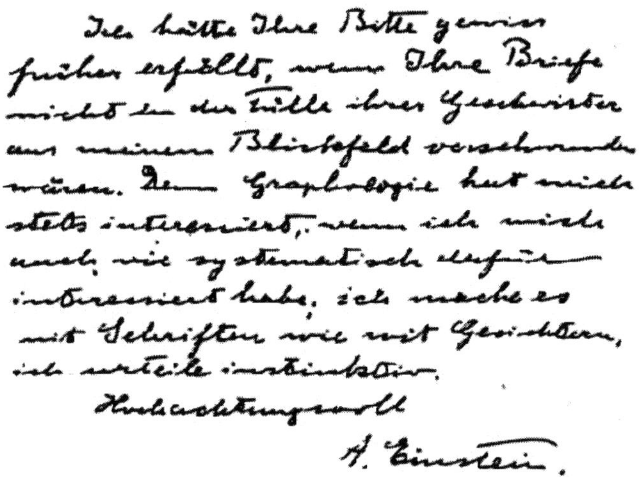

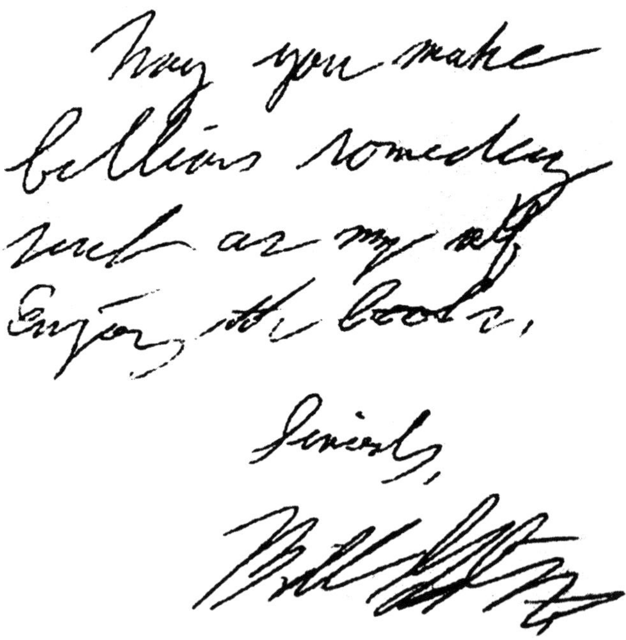

How does it feel to write like a monarch (Queen Elizabeth II), or a genius (Albert Einstein) or a billionaire software architect (Bill Gates)? You could do this exercise with anyone's handwriting and feel similar feelings and sensations, for we are all individuals dealing with our own individual issues. You walk a unique journey – the hidden 'netivot' without markers or signposts – and your circumstances and the themes and issues of your life are there to help you and no-one else. That's why stepping into someone else's handwriting can give you insights into their issues but it cannot solve yours.

Handwriting is protean – being and becoming

Chrysippus of Soli (c.280–c.207 BCE) used the metaphor of the rolling cylinder whose motion is initiated by a push but whose continued rolling is the result of the cylinder's shape to demonstrate the idea that if we work on ourselves and we change our shape, then our fate will change.[2] If we link that with the twentieth-century gesture-language studies of David McNeill, who argues that gestures are active participants in both speaking and thinking, and that the shape and timing of gestures depends on what speakers see and what they take to be unique in the context,[3] then we start to understand that thinking, gesture and shape are all interconnected. Like an orchestra, if a conductor changes the gestures he or she makes, the orchestra will change the music they make.

We also make gestures on paper through our handwriting. We write what we think, but also how we feel and so handwriting comes to express who we are. Thus changing what we feel will change our handwriting and changing our handwriting can help to change how we feel. This shape-changing or protean quality makes handwriting a brilliant tool and a perfect bridge between an astrological chart and the lived experience – being (the chart) and becoming (the handwriting). When we alter the way we make strokes we are altering the way we view life. We gain a window into ourselves. Such attentive application allows us to be consciously involved with our own transformational process. Your pen and your handwriting become your instruments for bringing changes into your life.

How we manage to survive

What is it in our natal charts that our handwriting echoes?

We all endeavour to keep our lives balanced. If we are happy, our writing will contain happy shapes. If we are sad or upset or frustrated, the handwriting

---

2. A.A. Long and D.N. Sedley, eds, *The Hellenistic Philosophers, Volume 1: Translations of the Principal Sources with Philosophical Commentary*, (Cambridge: Cambridge University Press, 1987), p.388.
3. David McNeill, *Gesture and Thought* (Chicago: Chicago University Press, 2007).

will show this, too. Most of us attempt to keep our lives in balance, and we can see this as reflecting our attempt to balance the different needs and drives of our natal chart. However, what is out of balance in your life at any given time will be revealed in your handwriting.

Everything in our natal chart wants expression. Just as we physically grow at different rates, so we all develop at different speeds mentally, emotionally, psychically and spiritually. So some parts of us are more mature than others, and all of these conscious and unconscious levels will seek expression in the handwriting.

Huge life changes begin with one small alteration. We tend to think of change as monumental, yet how many great plans are dreamed into being over breakfast? It is the small gesture that heralds large change and you can bring this change into your life through as simple a motion as consciously changing a handwritten stroke.

This is an important basic understanding. History tells us that when too many changes are made too rapidly, civilizations collapse. Any garden wants a light shower of rain to make things grow, not a deluge, and the most effective changes will come from small conscious adjustments integrated one step at a time. Remember, however, that making even a small change in your handwriting is making a contract with yourself and as a result, two things will happen:

If you make changes in your handwriting, change will happen. If you do not want any changes in your life, do not make any changes in your handwriting.

When you decide to make a change in your handwriting then you must keep your end of the bargain. We know this from fairy tales and myths. In *Rumplestiltskin*, the miller's daughter promises the manikin her first child if he will help her to spin straw into gold but when this event comes to pass and she realizes her foolishness, the degree of difficulty for her to extract herself from this bargain is far higher than she anticipates. Changes don't usually come with bells and whistles, although I have known this to happen. More often they come as small nuances, tiny synchronicities, seemingly small coincidences. They are lights in the field and they draw us towards them, and if we refuse to move in that direction then life at the very least constricts, at its worst it implodes. Bernadette Brady uses the metaphor of Khnum, who captures the small emergent filaments of silt that rise from the Nile and, by shaping them into animate forms, creates life on his potter's wheel.[4] Such animate forms are the patterns that we want to materialize in our present circumstances.

---

4. Bernadette Brady, *Astrology, a place in chaos* (Bournemouth: The Wessex Astrologer, 2006), pp.10-11.

Like emails from our unconscious, we can tell how well we are managing to survive in the writing we create.

Procedure

This book is about creating new shapes with the art that you make and, as a result, making new conscious choices for yourself about how you will go out and meet life, how you will co-create the unmade future that is still emerging. However, like any major task in life, we work on discrete sections of our handwriting at any given period. So experiment with different letters and strokes and find which ones you write easily and which are difficult. They will give you a great deal of information about yourself. Bear in mind that most of us avoid change for, as a general rule, we do not handle it well. So if you wish to alter your life, choose just one new stroke and make a pact with yourself that you will work on this and this alone in your handwriting for the next month. That way as each new stroke becomes incorporated, you will slowly usher in the changes you want to make.

Our chart is the 'being' – what we are to begin with – but our lives, our choices and our handwriting are the 'becoming' – what we make of our chart. Handwriting is a tool to help the 'becoming'.

2

The Landscape of Handwriting

The *Sefer Yetzirah*, the sacred ancient book linking handwriting with co-creation, describes the universe as being fashioned from Space, Time and Soul. So if one wishes to influence the physical universe (space) one can make use of the physical shape of the letters which, according to the *Sefer Yetzirah*, are the sacred building blocks of the world.[1] On a personal level we can apply this approach to the letters of our own handwriting. As we write we are both creating and reflecting who we are, how we think and what we feel. In handwriting we are focusing on Space. By altering Space we know from the *Sefer Yetzirah* that we can then alter Time and Soul. This means that, by changing the letters of our handwriting, we change the quality of our lives.

If we consider how we write, then a page of handwriting can be viewed as a landscape, a map of the Space. The way the letters structure the space on the page tells us how we inhabit that landscape, and as a result how we understand the time and spiritual dimension of the world in which we live. We are in effect forming a constructed landscape via the shapes of our handwriting. Such a landscape will include three areas formed by the gestures we make: those that sweep upwards away from the body, those that maintain steadiness, and those that flow downwards towards the body.

Upper region: the mountains

This is the area of your handwriting that contains gestures that sweep upwards, literally away from the body, seen in the heights of the letters 'b' 'd' 'f' 'h' 'k' 'l' 't'. These parts of the letters reach into the peaks and mountains of your life. As sites closest to heaven, mountains are traditionally places of inspiration. We look up at mountains in awe and wonder, and some of us set ourselves the challenge of climbing them, offsetting the effort taken to trek there by the view we anticipate

---

1. Aryeh Kaplan, *Sefer Yetzirah, the Book of Creation*, Revised Edition (San Francisco: Red Wheel/ Weiser, 1997), pp.19-21.

The Landscape of Handwriting

The Mountains - Where We Seek Inspiration

b d f h k l t

those parts of the letters formed by movements
away from our body, up the page,
ascending to the mountain peaks.

Show us our mind and our imagination,
our intellect, our philosophical or spiritual concepts,
the sphere of reflection and meditation,
of abstraction, and speculation which is not subject
to material considerations:
our hopes, plans, aspirations,
and how we reach for our goals.

The Plains - Where We Live

a c e i m n o r s u
v w x z

those parts of the letters formed in the middle path
of our writing that move it forward,
providing the central plateau.

Show us our approach to work and daily life
and how we relate to the mundane reality
of the world around us:
our partners, children, family, animal friends.

The Valleys - Where We Feel

f g j p q y z

those parts of the letters formed by movements
towards our body, down the page,
to the depths of our world.

Show us how we live with our feelings:
our primal instincts and emotions,
and our attitude towards relationships and sexuality.
In some cases this area can show irrationality,
depression and the desire for solitude,
things of which we are unconscious or seek to hide.

enjoying once we reach the peaks. Such a view gives us the large sweep, the big picture, the wide horizon, the result of struggle. So this part of your handwriting describes your mind and your imagination, your intellect and your philosophical concepts. These letters tell you about the mountains of your lives, how you reach up towards your hopes, your plans, your aspirations and, most importantly, how you reach for your goals. It is where you seek to reflect and meditate and so where and how you seek inspiration. Thus it describes the spiritual attributes of your life. It is also the place of abstract thinking and speculation which is not subject to material considerations.

Does your handwriting overall contain letters that display ambition and inspiration? Are they in proportion to the rest of your letters? Are they parts of letters that would normally reach upwards in this way? Is there anything in your natal chart that might indicate the desire for achievement, such as planets in your 10th house or Sun-Saturn, or the need to seek or offer others inspiration, such as an emphasis of planets in fire signs?

Example: A mountain-climber

This is an example of a student's work; the exercise was to discuss his own Ascendant-Descendant axis. Observe the loops on the letters 'h', 'f' and 'l' and how letters with stems, such as 'b', 'd' and 't', rise high into these mountainous regions. In most cases these loops and stems are in proportion to the rest of the letter.

This suggests someone who plans for and reaches for his goals and uses abstract thinking and speculation to achieve this. I have drawn in the tramlines so you can see this movement up into the mountainous regions.

Middle region: the plains

This is the area of your handwriting that touches the earth and thus creates the walls and structures of your life, seen in the letters 'a' 'c' 'e' 'm' 'n' 'o' 'r' 's' 'u' 'v' 'w' 'x' 'z'. These parts of the letters inhabit the world of the plains and describe how you maintain your routines through steadiness and form, where the practicality of your life is expressed.

This is the area of your handwriting which illuminates your approach to your work and daily life, and how you relate to your world – your children, family, partners, and animal friends – the mundane reality of your life.

Does your handwriting overall contain letters that offer this practicality? How well-grounded are you, suggested by the shape of your letters? Are they in proportion to the rest of the letters? Are there parts of these letters that reach into the mountains or flood outside the practical region? Is there anything in your natal chart that might indicate how you achieve this stability, such as an emphasis of planets in fixed or earth signs?

Example: a plains dweller

The writing of this student, who lives and works on a farm, is located almost entirely in this central region of her landscape. Letters that sweep up into the mountains such as 'l' and 'f' inhabit the practical world, suggesting someone who is highly focused on the functional and the manifestation of their day to day routines, one who is reliable, purposeful, wants to get things done and has little time for setting goals that fall outside common-sense and realism.

le an essay on hydrostatic balance, which made him famous that In his mid twenties he began research in earnest and developed several theories that are still in use today. He was the first person to convert the recently invented telescope to onical purposes. He then made several discoveries, i.e. that the sun moon was irregular and not smooth as hitherto supposed; he also c

The lowlands: the valleys

This is the area of your handwriting that contains gestures that surge downwards, taking the lower path underneath the body of the letter, seen in the sweeps of the letters 'f' 'g' 'j' 'p' 'q' 'y' 'z'. This movement, literally towards your body as you write on the page, mirrors movement into yourself, the part you access when you respond emotionally, whether through happiness or by being disturbed at some level. The hidden, the unconscious, and the world of dreams and shadows are also places that offer you insights, often buried, regarding family concerns or unresolved emotional issues.

These letters that travel into this part of your handwriting describe your primal instincts and emotions, hence your attitude towards relationships, sexuality and emotional security. In some cases this area can show irrationality, depression and the desire for solitude, things you seek to hide or of which you are unconscious.

Does your handwriting overall contain letters that embrace emotion? Are they in proportion to the rest of the letters? Are they over-emphasized or non-existent? Is there anything in your natal chart that might emphasize emotions, such as planets in water signs, or sexuality, such as Mars-Pluto, or indicate hidden family issues, such as 12th house planets or unaspected planets?

Example: a lowlands dweller

This student's writing has extremely long loops on her 'f', 'p' and 'y' letters, extending deep into the valleys of her world. This suggests that there are emotional issues with which she is still struggling or of which she is unaware. Long loops like this can also indicate someone who feels ineffective and so seeks privacy and seclusion.

I prefer to write with a pencil! Softer, less permanent than pen, which seems to ossify my thoughts prematurely. Rubbing out still leaves an impression, so my original phrasing can still be recorded; yet the overall impression of the page is of less ... than occurs with the crossing-out ...

The universal traveller - f

The letter 'f' is the only letter whose parts extend upwards to the mountains, downwards into the valleys and completes in the plains, so it holds a unique position in the alphabet, one of sacred balance, travelling across our entire being.

At this stage just be aware that this letter moves through the entire landscape and it will be discussed more fully in Chapter 4.

Take a moment now to review the handwriting samples in Chapter One and decide where the focus lies? How practical was Einstein? How emotional is Bill Gates? How inspirational is Queen Elizabeth II?

Now take a look at your own handwriting and decide where the focus of your handwriting lies.

In summary...

The landscape of our handwriting reflects the inner and outer landscapes of our experiences to date. This landscape covers three terrains - our mountains and our aspirations, our plains and our practical reality, and our valleys and intuitive, instinctual sides. Corresponding to this, the shape of written language that uses the Roman alphabet allows us to express ourselves using the three terrains. This suggests that for our life to develop in a way that is progressively more mature and aware, it is appropriate for our handwriting to include a balance between what we dream (our mountains and our aspirations), how we make those dreams a reality (our plains and practical reality) and the passion we invest in experiencing them (our valleys and intuitive, instinctual sides). This balance between mountains, plains and valleys can also be found in our chart.

As the *Sefer Yetzirah* tells us – change the space, change the time, change the soul.

3

Methodology

The Patterns of Handwriting as a way of Approaching the Astrology

If writing is our landscape, then the layout on the page is the way we dance on that landscape. Handwriting presents us with a visual perspective of the way we view and move through our life. The page forms the microcosmic bounds of our world.

Handwriting takes the twenty six letters of the alphabet and places them across the page in an order that makes sense of our thoughts. This idea that handwriting can tell us about a person has been around for a long time. Confucius (551-479 BCE) noted that 'Handwriting can infallibly show whether it comes from a person who is noble-minded or from one who is vulgar.' Aristotle (384-322 BCE) wrote that 'Spoken words are the symbols of mental experience and written words are the symbols of the spoken words. Just as all men do not have the same speech sounds, neither do they all have the same writing.' The Roman historian Suetonius Tranquillus (69–122 CE) in his *De Vitae Caesurum*, said of Emperor Augustus: 'He does not separate his words — I do not trust him.'

What did they see in the handwriting that made them write such words? Just as when we meet a stranger we can often make a correct assessment about what their Ascendant might be, so we can look at someone's handwriting and get an overall sense about the person. We can do this because handwriting reflects who and what we are, just like the chart. On the personal level we can think of handwriting as a piece of art we unconsciously create in order to communicate with ourselves. It is our imagination made visible, a way of anchoring our thoughts, feelings, emotions and responses onto the page. The words we write and the sentences we create produce art which is a mirror image of us and how we place ourselves in the world and therefore, by correlation, our handwriting mirrors our chart.

Checklist for handwriting

This checklist is designed to alert you to the major areas to focus upon when looking at handwriting. Many books on graphology will consider handwriting as a way of observing a person's psyche. My intention is to alert you to the gestures we make that reflect what is going on for us in present time and how to map those issues to the natal chart. Once you understand **what** you are looking at, then your knowledge of astrology will alert you as to **where** the issue lies in the natal chart, as well as inform you of the range of possibilities that are contained within the chart. There is a summary checklist at the end of this chapter.

1. Margins are our time and space — the way we move on the page is the way we move through life.

We come from a culture that writes horizontally from left to right with a generally accepted rightward slant and these horizontal lines move vertically from the top of the page downwards. As we place our thoughts on the page, we leave what we have written to the left of us, moving towards new ideas and thoughts on the right. As we move down the page we create a history of thinking. So there are four directions we encounter when we write. We begin on the left hand side of the page and we move to the right. We begin at the top of the page and we move down to the bottom of the page. Have a look at a page of your own handwriting. How does your handwriting sit on the page? Do you begin hard up against the left hand side of the page or almost in the middle of the page? Do you run out of space as you reach the right hand side or do you give yourself plenty of room? Are your margins wide or tight? Look closely as this will tell you how you relate to your temporal and physical environment:

(i) The left hand side of the page designates the past, how you feel about it, how much of an impact or hold it still has on you, how well you leave what is completed behind you, and how you utilize what you have learnt from the past as your resources in the present. **Margins that hug the left side of the page** suggest someone who is tied to the past and allows it to dominate their present, unconsciously fearful of letting go of their history and thus enslaved to it, someone who does not seek personal contact and who tends to lean on the past for security and answers. **A wide left margin** indicates someone who has a desire to get on with life leaving the past behind, so that the past becomes memories rather than an unconscious web constraining the future.

(ii) The right hand side of the page signifies the future, your ability to plan, your expectations, your enthusiasm for what lies ahead of you, and how you wish to be involved in the environment and the world around you. **Margins that hug the right side of the page** suggest either a forthright decision-maker, someone who uninhibitedly reaches out to the future, or else someone who is over-eager, rushing headlong into situations instead of allowing them to emerge, lacking tact and invading others' privacy. **A wide right margin** indicates someone who is immensely fearful of the future and of commitment and who will hold back rather than move forward to meet life's challenges and achieve their goals.

(iii) The top of the page indicates personal space, how considerate and respectful you are in your connections with others and where you begin your conversations with them. **Margins that hug the top of the page** suggest someone who dives into discussion with enthusiasm due to familiarity or who comes from a space of self-centredness and with little regard for other people's states of being. **A wide top margin** indicates someone who is thoughtful and courteous of others and who recognizes their need for space.

(iv) The bottom of the page represents how you move forward with your life. The more this is filled, the more passionate you are in telling your story. However, it is also connected with preparation and scheduling and, depending on how cramped or crushed your handwriting becomes as it reaches the bottom of the page, it also tells you how well you handle your resources of time and space. **Margins that hug the bottom of the page** suggest someone who eagerly fills their world and wants to communicate it and, depending on how tightly this squashes the lower margin of the page, will tell you how well they balance enthusiasm and planning. **A wide lower margin** in a continuing piece of handwriting indicates someone who is reticent and who may not reveal all there is to say.

The closer the writing is to the top of the page,
the more familiar the writer feels they are to the recipient,
or it can indicate self-centredness.

**The left hand
side of the page**
designates the past, its impact,
its current hold and how well you leave
what is completed behind you.

**The right hand
side of the page**
signifies the future, your enthusiasm
for what lies ahead of you,
and how you wish to be involved
in the world.

Margins

are our time and space –

the way we move on the page

reflects the way we move through life.

The closer the writing is to the bottom of the page,
the more information the writer feels they have to communicate,
or they may lack planning ability.

Figure 1: A diminishing left hand margin indicates someone who wants to be independent of their past but is pulled back by it. No lower margin shows enthusiasm as well as lack of planning.

Figure 2: These are narrow but balanced margins.

Youth is not a time of life. It is a state of mind. It is a temper of the will, a quality of the imagination, a vigour of the emotions, a predominance of courage over timidity, of the appetite for adventure over love of ease.

Nobody grows old by merely living a number of years. People grow old only by deserting their ideals. Years wrinkle the skin, but to give up enthusiasm wrinkles the soul.

Whether 60 or 16, there is in every being's heart the love of wonder, the sweet amazement at the stars and star-like things and thoughts, the undaunted challenge of events, the unfailing childlike appetite for what-next, and the joy in the game of living.

You are as young as your faith, as old as your doubt; as young as your self confidence, as old as your fear; as young as your hope, as old as your despair.

So long as your heart receives messages of beauty, hope, cheer, grandeur and power from the earth, from men and from the Infinite, so long are you young.

Live everyday of your life as you expect to live forever.

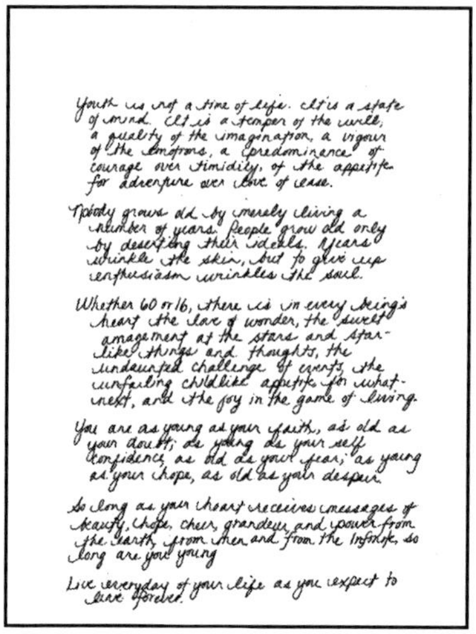

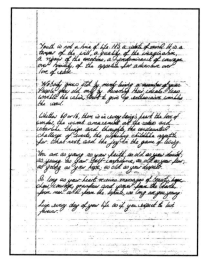

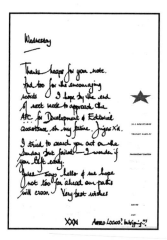

Figure 3: The wide top margin shows respect for the recipient. However, the zigzag left hand margin shows the person has conflicting impulses. As another woman with this characteristic in her handwriting put it: 'I try to go forward and I'm pulled back to the past. It's a root I have to cut.'

Youth is not a time of life. It's a state of mind. It is a temper of the will, a quality of the imagination, a vigour of the emotions, a predominance of courage over timidity, of the appetite for adventure over love of ease.

Nobody grows old by merely living a number of years. People grow old only by deserting their ideals. Years wrinkle the skin. But to give up enthusiasm wrinkles the soul.

Whether 60 or 16, there is in every being's heart the love of wonder, the sweet amazement at the stars and starlike things and thoughts, the undaunted challenge of events, the unfailing childlike appetite for what next, and the joy in the game of living.

You are as young as your faith, as old as your doubt; as young as your self-confidence, as old as your fear; as young as your hope, as old as your despair.

So long as your heart receives messages of beauty, hope, cheer, courage, grandeur and power from the Earth, from man and from the Infinite, so long are you young.

Live every day of your life as if you expect to live forever.

Figure 4: Written on lined paper and with the left hand margin hugging the guideline, this indicates a person who follows rules and regulations to the letter. The wide top margin reveals respect for the recipient of the letter.

Wednesday

Thanks heaps for your note. And too for the encouraging words. I hope by the end of next week to approach the AFC for Development & Editorial assistance on my feature. Fingers X'd.

I tried to search you out on the Sunday but failed — I wonder if you left early.

Jules says hello & we hope not too far ahead our paths will cross. Very best wishes

XXX Astro Locos? Intriguing!!!

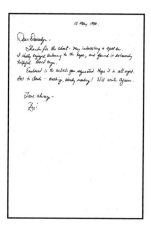

Figure 5: A straight left margin points to a person who is disciplined and grounded.

15 May 1990.

Dear Darrelyn -

Thanks for the chart - very interesting & spot on. I really enjoyed listening to the tape, and found it extremely helpful. Good ways.

Enclosed is the article you requested. Hope it is all right. Got to dash - meetings, bloody meetings! Will write again.

Love always -

Bi

Figure 6: A narrow top margin indicates familiarity.

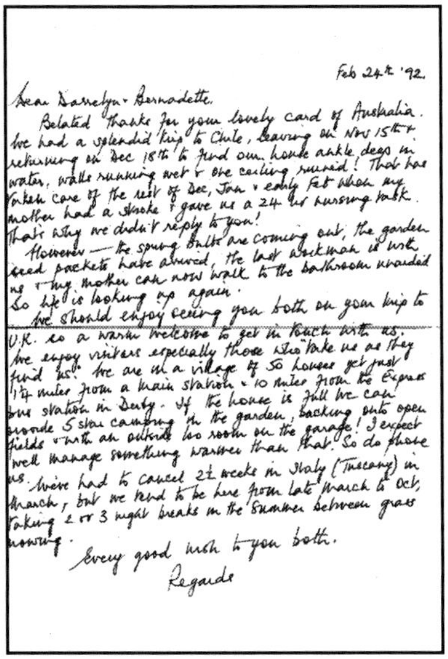

Feb 24th '92.

Dear Darrelyn & Bernadette.
Belated thanks for your lovely card of Australia.
We had a splendid trip to Chile, leaving on Nov 15th &
returning on Dec 18th to find our house ankle deep in
water, walls running wet & one ceiling ruined! That has
taken care of the rest of Dec, Jan & early Feb when my
mother had a stroke & gave us a 24 hr nursing task.
That's why we didn't reply to you!
However — the spring bulbs are coming out, the garden
seed packets have arrived, the last workman is with
us & my mother can now walk to the bathroom unaided
So life is looking up again.
We should enjoy seeing you both on your trip to
U.K. so a warm welcome to get in touch with us.
We enjoy visitors especially those who take us as they
find us. We are in a village of 50 houses yet just
1¼ miles from a main station & 10 miles from the Express
bus station in Derby. If the house is full we can
provide 5 star camping in the garden, backing onto open
fields & with an outside loo room on the garage! I expect
we'll manage something warmer than that. So do phone
us. We've had to cancel 2½ weeks in Italy (Tuscany) in
March, but we tend to be here from late March to Oct,
taking 2 or 3 night breaks in the summer between grass
mowing.
Every good wish to you both.
Regards

Figure 7: No left hand margin suggests a highly insecure person whose fears stem from early life experiences, someone who is deeply tied to the past.

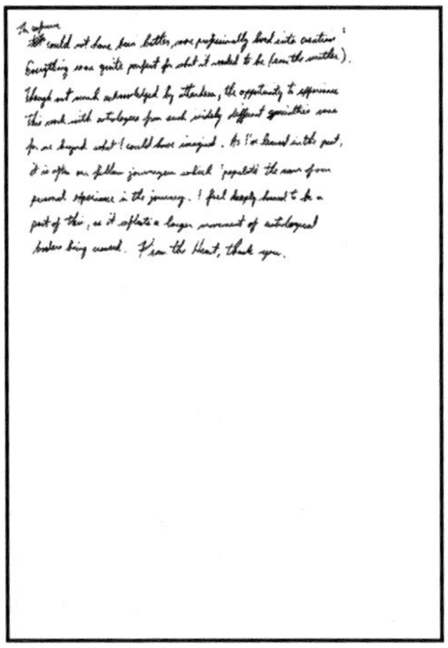

Figure 8: This wide right hand margin suggests a person who is immensely fearful of the future and of commitment and who stops short of reaching their goals.

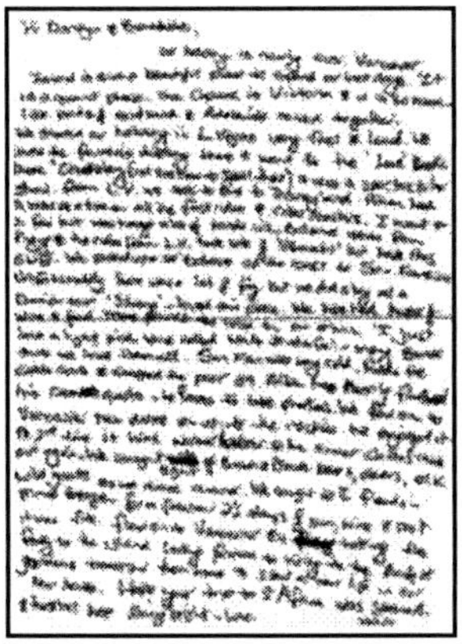

Figure 9: No margins all round indicates someone who leaves no room for other people and may have trouble seeing things from other people's perspectives.

2. Line and word spacing provides our processing framework — the space we give to our thinking.

Letters weren't always connected. As children, learning for the first time how to hold a writing implement and to train our muscles to make marks on the page, we printed the letters separately from each other.

This corresponds with our mental development and one of the abilities we gain through being educated is to learn how to link impressions and concepts. As Mendel points out, 'connected' writing parallels our ability to connect our thoughts and ideas and allows us to write faster.[1] If we know how we connect our thoughts, we not only know how we think, we also become acquainted with the way we associate with the people around us, how we relate, socialize and network physically, mentally, emotionally, psychically, and spiritually. As well, maturity offers us the opportunity to be independent of what has been learnt by rote at school and to contribute original ways of thinking. Some of us find this easy to do, and the fluidity or creativity with which we do this will also be articulated in the natal chart. Others may find the mores of education, religion or peer group too big an obstacle to overcome and will continue to follow a pattern of handwriting that comes from the past, rigidly enforced in our formative years and glued to the present by a fear of letting go.

What is the spacing like between your lines and between words? Do you allow new thoughts into your thinking or crowd others with your own thoughts?

Spacing within words is generally said to be the width of the letter 'a'. When all the letters are connected, this denotes either a person with logical, systematic thinking or someone with rigid thinking, depending on other indicators in the handwriting. Remember, one handwriting trait is not enough to make a judgement.

ability   *amazement*

When only some of the letters are connected, this suggests an artistic or intuitive thinker, self-reliant and independent, resourceful and creative. The person allows space within their own thinking patterns for new thoughts, whether from others or from within themselves.

Euphoria   *successful*

---

1. Mendel, Alfred O. *Personality in Handwriting* (North Hollywood: Newcastle Publishing Co., Inc. 1990), p.163.

When most of the letters are disconnected, this suggests independence or egocentric thinking, someone who is inspirational or one who is careless of the feelings of others and rides roughshod over them. In its more difficult expression this can indicate those who feel isolated and lonely, moody, and even impatient.

stunning   important   insight

The spaces between words are the natural pauses of thought. A harmonious distance between words is said to be the space of a letter 'm' or 'n'.

thanks for your lovely card

When handwriting is tight and cramped it allows no room for self-expression. It indicates someone who needs a great deal of people contact due to a fear of being alone but when they are with others, they will talk non-stop, revealing a mind that is closed to other people's ideas.

Inconsistent distances between words point toward inconsistencies in social interactions, oscillating between spontaneity and reticence.

The spaces between the lines of our writing indicate how we relate to the outside world. When words and lines are visibly separated they show clear thinking, an ability to organize, motivate and maintain drive towards a goal without being diverted, as well as a balanced outlook on life.

thank you for the beautiful
angel who brought your
Christmas and New Year
greetings. We wish you
a wonderful New Year
with even more stars,

A harmonious distance is felt to be the interval where the lines can be read clearly and where the valley loops of one line avoid the mountains of the handwriting below. If the lines crash into each other in this way, the person may harbour some conscious or unconscious aggression and/or lack diplomacy.

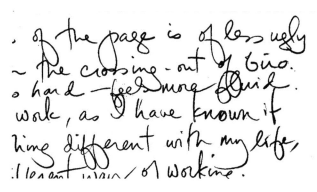

3. The three landscapes give us our orientation in space — where does our focus lie? (See Chapter Two: The Landscapes of Writing).

4. Letter slant reveals the compass directions of our life — how we reach out or pull away from life.

(i) **Letters leaning towards the left.** It is often thought that people who write with their left hand will naturally write with a left-handed slant. However,

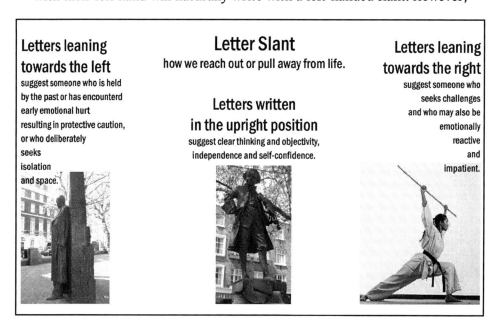

Letters leaning towards the left suggest someone who is held by the past or has encounterd early emotional hurt resulting in protective caution, or who deliberately seeks isolation and space.

Letter Slant
how we reach out or pull away from life.

Letters written in the upright position suggest clear thinking and objectivity, independence and self-confidence.

Letters leaning towards the right suggest someone who seeks challenges and who may also be emotionally reactive and impatient.

this is not the case. A left-handed slant is indicative of someone who is held by the past or has encountered early emotional hurt resulting in protective caution or who deliberately seeks isolation and space. It can also be found in the handwriting of people who are highly talented and creative but who underestimate their ability or who lack confidence in themselves and thus may be shy and sensitive and hide their feelings. What may be guarded and defensive may be interpreted incorrectly as detached and indifferent.

she will be dealing with the packed energy of a relationship which is experienced as lower than the... Two of them.

If he was showered with material of his position, he probably became accustomed to a luxury life from

Delighted by your continuing success. Really proud of you both. Have a good time in '95.

Love from,

(ii) **Letters written in the upright position** suggest clear thinking and objectivity, independence and self-confidence. Such people tend to think before they act and thus work well under pressure, remaining calm in a crisis. They will take on positions of responsibility, as well as become accomplished at working on their own.

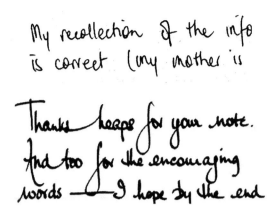

My recollection of the info is correct (my mother is

Thanks heaps for your note. And too for the encouraging words — I hope by the end

(iii) Letters leaning towards the right suggest someone who seeks challenge and may also be emotionally reactive and impatient. It is a sign of sociability, and such people are often affectionate and outgoing, well-suited to working with people.

Finally we have acquital!

Attached is your Planning Consent. If you wish me to carry out the Building Regulation work, please let me know and I will put it in my work schedule.

In extreme cases if the letter slants too far to the right, then such people may be over-dependent on and influenced by the opinions of others.

(iv) Letters that adhere to the lines of the page suggest a pressing need to conform, to 'toe the line', to be seen as behaving acceptably and fitting in with everyone else.

heart The love of wonder; The at The stars and starlike the The undaunted challenge of unfailing childlike appetite

Letters that sit above line suggest someone who will not be dominated or commanded by their world but prefers to use their initiative and original thinking.

Study compositions

Help the client to gain a broad indepth understanding of himself within the world he is living in.

5. Line slant reveals your confidence – what you believe will be the outcome of your ventures.

(i) **Lines that slope upwards** indicate optimism, enthusiasm, happy to work hard and a strong desire for self-expression.

Life drawing 14.2.07.
Measurement of Proportion

- RELATIONAL DECISIONS
Keep an wholistic encounter with the figure.
To move from the GENERAL to the PARTICULAR

(ii) **Lines that slope downwards** suggest mental or physical exhaustion, as well as depression or pessimism brought on by ill-health.

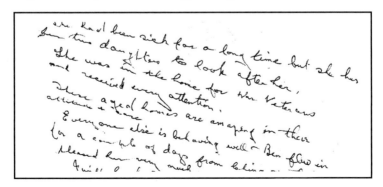

(iii) **Lines that form concave patterns** suggest someone who begins a venture reluctantly but gains enthusiasm as the project continues and will persevere to the end.

Further to today's telephone conversation, please find enclosed

(iv) **Lines that form convex patterns** suggest someone who begins ventures with enthusiasm but lacks the vitality or drive to complete them.

So long as your heart receives messages of beauty, hope, cheer, courage, grandeur and power from the earth, from men and from the Infinite, so long are your young.

6. The size of the letters we write is the footprint we make — how we tread upon the earth.

Large handwriting conveys flamboyance. Depending on what else is in the handwriting, it can also cover feelings of inadequacy.

I did so in a far more Conservative way than my private life would have suggested.
I was in the middle of one of these public phases when my daughter was

Small handwriting is often found where accuracy, precision and concentration are required, areas like research, science, mathematics or computer technology.

If so, how? *In much the same way as above*

Someone who usually writes in a large hand may, at times of intense focus, find they are writing smaller, for as the mind zeroes in on particular ideas and concepts the hand involuntarily restricts its movement and the result is smaller writing.

the questions are beyond my development

However, extremely small writing in the plains landscape may also indicate someone covering an inadequate ego, or a fear of their emotions. Between five and ten percent of people whose writing is perpetually small feel small in importance.[2]

Exceptionally small or microscopic writing is an extreme form of small handwriting and any extreme found in handwriting indicates a corresponding extreme in behaviour. It is only possible to write this small and retain legibility by focusing intensely and shutting out all external stimuli. For such a person, at the time when they are writing nothing exists but themselves, their ideas and thoughts. This is a time when they are highly introverted, focused deep within their world and oblivious to all and sundry. There are two distinct types of people who write with exceptionally small writing: the first is that of profound thinkers, seen for example in the small regular writing of Albert Einstein; the second is that of disturbed persons, such as Charlotte and Branwell Brontë who, as children, wrote many of their stories of Angria on tiny sheets of paper in nearly microscopic handwriting, indicating that they were compensating for an almost unbearably constricted childhood. In this category, when the handwriting is consistently confined to small movements and restricted in space on the paper, it indicates someone who is continually shrinking inside themselves. For such people, microscopic handwriting reflects their preference for their own company because they are fearful others will see them for who they believe themselves to be — nothing but an empty vessel.

Above: The handwriting of Albert Einstein.

---

2. Andrea McNichol and Jeffrey A. Nelson, *Handwriting Analysis: Putting It to Work for You*, (New York: McGraw-Hill Professional, 1994), p.144.

Above: A page with scale from *The Secret* showing the microscopic handwriting of Charlotte Bronte.[3]

All capitals as a form of communication are like a wall of bricks across the page. This belongs to the person who is fearful of allowing any excess energy, emotion, or feeling into their life, and is apprehensive of a natural spontaneity which may never have been adequately modelled for them as a child. Focused mainly into the mundane plains landscape, all-capitals writing walls up a person's emotions and chains their feelings. When someone uses block printing consistently in their

3. http://mulibraries.missouri.edu/specialcollections/exhibits/brontemanuscript.htm- accessed October 2008.

written communication, this is usually a sign that the person has endured deep suffering and pain at some stage of their life and has not found a secure environment in which to release it and heal. Consciously or unconsciously, they will always take a defensive position.

When someone writes as they were taught at school the statement they are making is that they wish to remain in or feel at their safest within the confines of convention. This impetus to obey convention can have a positive expression, seen in individuals who wish to serve their community with genuine humility, such as those who take up religious orders, become teachers, or move into the nursing or medical professions. However, an adult who continues to write exactly as they were taught at school exhibits a lack of development and individuality. These guy ropes of yesteryear unconsciously restrain and control their well of creativity and inspiration and inhibit their freedom of expression.

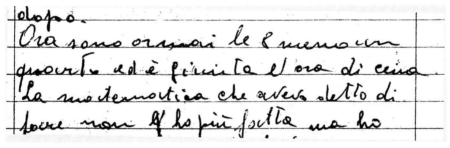

Here is an example of how handwriting changes with maturity:
1960 — aged 13 years:

1971 — aged 24 years:

2007 — aged 60 years:

ci hanno dato nel momento in cui
siamo reali. E per dato ___ la carta
del cielo è uno degli elementi,
forse il più importante perché

7. The way we connect the letters indicates the way we connect with others and how we find solutions to problems.

It is well-known to students in any field that the more senses we can bring to our understanding of an idea, the better it will stay in our memory. So writing notes and talking through our understanding helps this process immensely. This reflects a natural internal process: we write at the pace that we frame our thinking and hearing, and this reflects the way we connect letters together. We can make these connections in the following ways:

(i) Defining life sharply — angular writing employs the intellect.

An angle is formed by two lines or rays diverging from a common point, such as in the letter 'v', and it requires precision to create such a shape. So when this attribute is found consistently in handwriting, not just in the letter 'v', it signifies people who can see divergences and apply logic to their thinking. These are people with fine investigative abilities, well thought out methods and systems for examining or studying a subject, and a great amount of determination, and hence they often prefer to work alone. They also have sharp analytical or critical skills, self-discipline, persistence and strong willpower, as well as good planning and organizing abilities. They will happily take on a heavy workload, for they seem to flourish on challenges and difficulties, driving at them with a relentless edge.

Furthermore they are people who are trustworthy and reliable, for angles in a person's handwriting imply deep-seated principles about life, verging on the pedantic. Yet they also have a susceptibility to the strong emotions of people around them, resulting in the desire to shield themselves. This can, in turn, make them strongly judgmental, preferring to operate within rules and regulations, or to trust only that which is written down. This means they can also be rigid and intolerant in the way they approach life. Such lack of flexibility can give rise to anxiety and inner tension which can manifest as aggression. In its most difficult expression it can become a lack of compassion, obstinacy and insensitivity.

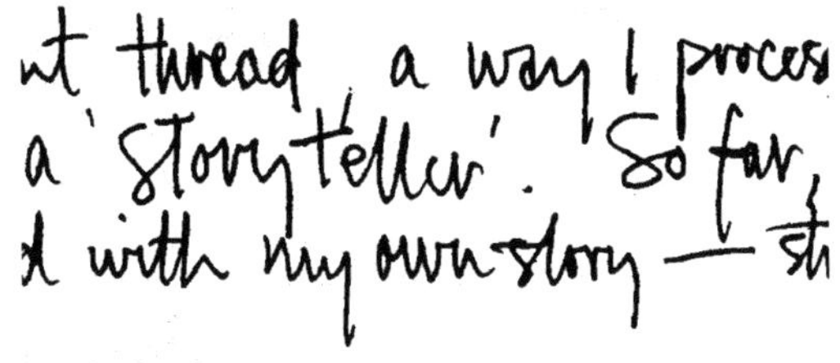

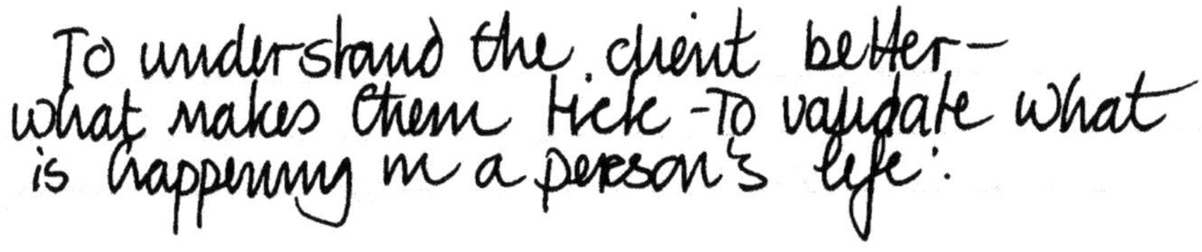

nt thread, a way I process
a 'storyteller'. So far,
I with my own story — sti

To understand the client better —
what makes them tick — To validate what
is happening in a person's life'.

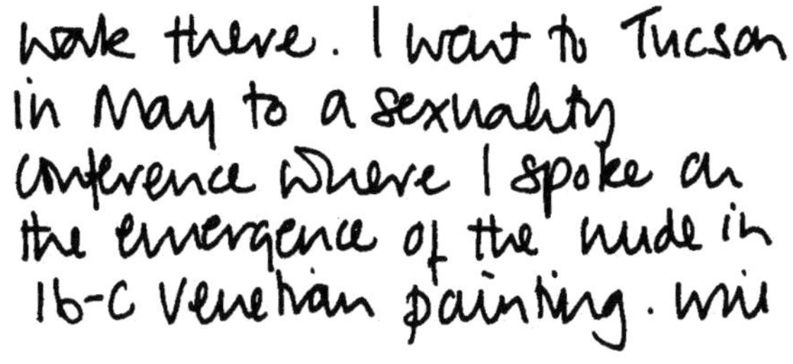

work there. I went to Tucson
in May to a sexuality
conference where I spoke on
the emergence of the nude in
16-c Venetian painting. wil

to understand themselves,
to achieve their aims
erstand the current & x

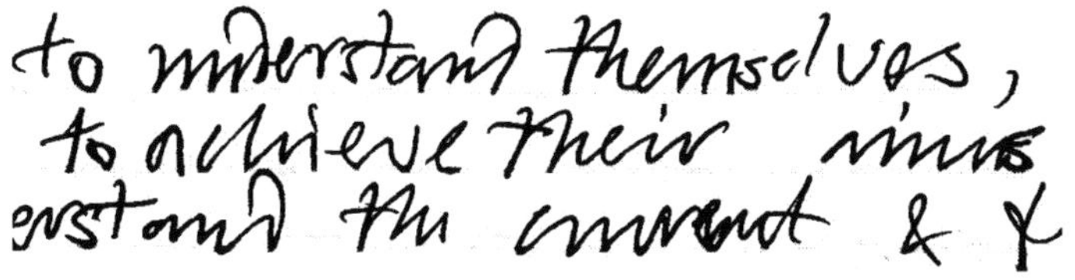

Angles belong in the practical plains region or in the goal-setting mountains. When angles find their way into our valleys, it causes difficulties, for logic is being applied to the area of instincts and emotions.

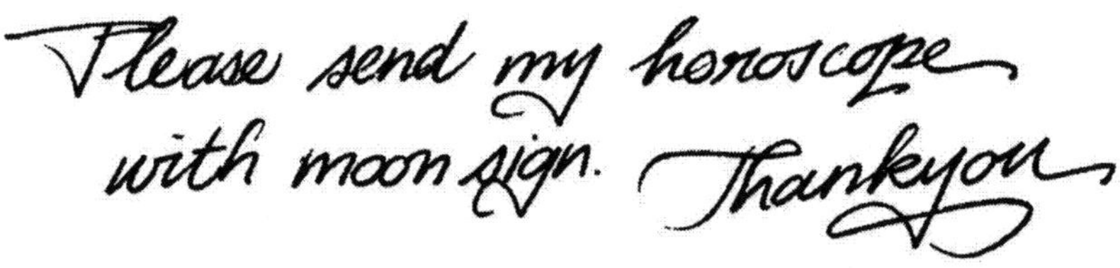

Please send my horoscope
with moon sign. Thankyou

In extreme cases angular writing can turn into compressed writing; writing that is so tightly squeezed together that it feels as if the life has been drained out of it, indicating someone who is totally closed to ideas and who has little opportunity to access their creativity.

(ii) Connecting with others - garland writing employs relating skills.
Garlands resemble a line of people holding hands together, so when this attribute of softly undulating 'u' shapes is found in handwriting it signifies people who reach out to others, who share thoughts and ideas, and who are open and receptive to ideas in return. Often called friendly writing, such people are empathic and considerate of the needs of others and this ability to put themselves into other people's shoes means they work well with human resources and social networks. However, they can also be too open and vulnerable to others' emotional states and may at times be considered naïve and gullible. Whilst this quality in a person's handwriting suggests they have the facility to negotiate and gain consensus, they do not necessarily possess the ability to confront and challenge and hence work best as part of a team, rather than in a leadership position.

treasured friends —
all best wishes for
a happy Christmas
and New Year
and love from

Thanks for your
letter and thoughts
my real birth time

When the undulations deepen to form a chalice, this can point to people who collect ideas, stories, people and objects.

If the shape is shallow, it can suggest someone who is too open, even superficial, someone who settles for compromise, who needs to be liked and accepted, and will do anything to avoid conflict and competition.

A variation is the **square garland**, the person whose mind is closed to new thoughts and ideas and who only reaches out to others when it falls within their own rigid structures. They often dismiss their intuition and maintain a narrow focus on life.

Turn left out of Crematorium to main road (A405)
Turn left on to A405
Go straight across (M1) to next

(iii) **Determination and focus — arcade writing employs protective structures.**

An arch is a curved structure which spans a space whilst supporting significant weight. It is the shape that forms bridges and aqueducts, so it carries weight and responsibility. It is also closed at the top, the inverse shape of the garland, so it does not allow breath into the letters and traps free expression. When this attribute is found in handwriting it signifies people who are restrained, self-absorbed and independent in behaviour and who maintain deep privacy. This may have resulted from an overbearing parent in childhood who repressed or blocked the child's spontaneity, resulting in their desire to be a diligent student. As a constructive thinker who works best with planning and structured learning, they will be drawn towards subjects that contain form and discipline and, as their handwriting suggests, they are often strongly-driven to achieve and create structures that last. As Sheila Lowe points out, architects and designers will tend to use the arcade form because they are drawn to the structural shape.[4]

d has not enabled me to required homework. I have to work my way through

---

4. Sheila Lowe, *The Complete Idiot's Guide to Handwriting Analysis* (New York: Alpha Books, 1999), p.213.

(iv) Empathy or invisibility — thread handwriting employs impressionability.

Threads appear in handwriting in the plains landscape as shapeless strands or pieces of cotton fibre, as if the writer has lost energy in inscribing them. Without clear definition, the reader is forced to make sense of the writing through the context or surrounding letters. When this attribute is found in handwriting it signifies people who apply this same lack of shape and form to their daily world, either using diplomacy as an evasive technique or being so sensitive to their surroundings that, like actors, they can take on the emotions and commitments of other people or characters. Hence they can either be talented, adaptable, and good at many things or, if the writing pressure is weak, lack personality, be seen as naïve and gullible, vacillating in their opinions, and suggestible.

8. The pressure we apply to our lives is the force of our personality — how we impress the page is how we impress the world.

The pressure we use in our handwriting indicates our life force and thus the exertion we bring to bear on our world.

Strong pressure indicates a person who approaches life with vitality, energy, will-power, and stamina. They will commit to projects and people and take things seriously.

Excessively heavy pressure can indicate someone under severe stress, perceiving criticism where none is intended, someone who may react first and ask questions afterwards.

Light pressure indicates people who are compliant, flexible and adaptable, responsive to the environment and empathic to people; in extreme cases this can indicate a lack of vitality or physical weakness.

Irregular pressure suggests inconsistency and unreliability.

9. How we begin and end words is how we step in, step out and step on from situations.

Word beginnings

The left-hand hook on this letter 't' in the mountain landscape suggests that this person's ambitions are being hooked into and inhibited by their past.

The extended trails on the left of these letters act as guy ropes, keeping them anchored to the practical world, and indicate that this person wants material safety and security.

Letters that begin in the valleys when they would not normally do so suggest resentment. The person places a fishing line down into their emotions, hauling them upwards involuntarily into their routine practicality.

In the example above, the valley hooks at the beginnings of the words 'my', 'inspiration' and 'was' pull unconscious emotions into this person's practical world.

Second

In this example, however, the valley hook on the letter 's' is implanted into this person's emotions with no outlet in the practical world, suggesting that, having suffered at the hands of others, they have learnt to defend themselves using blame and stinging verbal attacks.

Capital letters are a particular way of beginning words and are often used to create an impression. Since they designate the beginning of sentences, their size in proportion to the rest of the letters will be important. A balanced capital letter indicates a balanced self-esteem:

Every good wish to you both.

Over-large capitals indicate ambition and appear in the handwriting of people who seek rank and social standing. However, as the letters are written oversize, they indicate over-confidence and arrogance, someone who rides roughshod over others as a smokescreen against feelings of inadequacy and uncertainty or someone who feels so insecure they feel the need to bluff or inflate their ego.

Dear Darlyn

I'm enclosing resume. Maur next job is in its back to a year.

Dear Darcelyn,

Small capitals describe someone who is self-effacing, reserved, and prefers to remain in the background. In its more difficult expression it can also indicate someone who is insecure and self-doubting.

Understanding the person ; Why they do what they do .

English uses capital letters to point out important words. All sentences, proper names, titles of books, songs, stories, works of art, magazine articles, tests and other written materials, the capital letter 'I', the first word of a direct quotation and the titles of people when used with their names or in place of their names, all begin with a capital letter. Capitals found inside words, or misplaced capitals, are letters shaped out of sequence and so they can occur in the handwriting of someone who lacks formal education. However, more often the writer is someone who rebels against the rules of writing or grammatical correctness. Thus a misplaced capital suggests that the person in some way defies the norms and conventions of society and prefers to live outside the mainstream.

fRom

Capital R used in the middle of a word.

A spAce where mAjic cAn uNfold

Capital A and capital N used in the middle of words.

Word endings

horoscope

The extension on the end of the letter 'e' indicates this person reaches out to others and understands how to negotiate with others as a way of finding resolution and completion.

Please find enclosed cheque)

Both the letter 'd' at the end of 'enclosed' and the letter 'e' at the end of 'cheque' finish with a rising sweep into the mountains where normally they would end in the plains, suggesting a daydreamer or one who blurs their boundaries of practicality and goals and as a result may find it hard to complete things.

Affirmed and enlarged

The backwards lean of the letter 'd' pulls this person backwards away from others, suggesting the way they complete things is to withdraw.

10. Left luggage, attics and cellars — how we hide from ourselves or others.

Thirteen of the twenty-six letters we write contain areas that are completely closed. These are the letters 'a' 'b', 'd' 'f' 'g' 'h' 'j' 'k' 'l' 'o' 'p' 'q' and 'y'. These areas of containment, whether they are our fishing rods into the emotional valleys of our lives, ropes that reach up into the mountains of our imagination, or the dancing ovals or circles written into the practical area of our lives, are appropriate for the letter. When we attach extra elements to the letter, such as rings, circles, slashes or dashes that do not form part of the original shape of the letter, these become containers, storage places where emotions are able to hide or are buried. These can occur in all landscapes.

When containers appear on the left hand side of letters, since we write from left to right, they denote unconscious fears from past events that continue to have an effect in the present, preserving and trapping these issues in the body of the letter as they trap the person unconsciously in the past. Another expression of this type of residue is that the person may be hiding a personal vulnerability that has dogged them in the past, such as shyness and insecurity, and is now used as self-protection.

If this left luggage occurs in the mountain landscape, it creates trapped emotions connected with a person's imagination, spirituality and goals; if in the plains region, it creates trapped emotions connected with a person's daily life; if in the valleys, it creates trapped emotions connected with their instincts.

for

The letter 'o' in the example above contains a loop coming in from the left hand side, suggesting a vulnerability regarding the past and desire to hide it from others.

Extend

A loop in the final letter 't' of the example above indicates trapped emotions connected with the person's imagination, spirituality and goals.

arrived

An inflated letter 'd' stem, as in the example above, is also an indication of trapped emotions connected with the person's imagination, spirituality and goals. However, now it is linked with the circle of wholeness in the practical plains area, so it becomes a storage container for an accumulation of blame. The person feels so overburdened with having to attend to other people's needs and with so little time to reflect on their own ideas, plans, aspirations and goals that it can turn into unspoken resentment.

When containers appear on the right hand side of letters the person is gripped by issues connected with the future. This may be information they are holding about others in confidence or through accident which they cannot reveal. It may be personal information regarding a situation in which conflicting demands make it impossible to do one thing or the other, thus causing emotional distress that the person wants to keep hidden from others. It can also indicate intentional dishonesty to others, information that is purposefully concealed and, in extreme cases, depending on what else is in the handwriting, signifying hypocrisy, deception and manipulation.

love   *speak*

In the examples above, the letters 'o' in 'love' and 's' in 'speak' contain loops on the right-hand side.

When containers appear on both sides of a letter, then the person is double bound by both information they cannot reveal to others about themselves from the past and concerns about the future.

When an entire letter is encircled, or lassoed, then the person is being metaphorically strangled by that which they cannot speak. In these examples above, the letters 'a' in 'can' and 'o' in 'of' and 'you' are entirely encircled.

Loops on the left indicate the past: someone who hides their history, consciously or unconsciously, from themselves.

Loops on the right indicate other people: someone who withholds information from others; or someone who keeps confidences well.

The larger the loop, the more the person will avoid giving a complete answer.

> **With Compliments**
>
> Monday 13/12
>
> Darrelyn,
> my apologies for not forwarding the cheque earlier — an oversight on my behalf.
> Because my appointment is this week, I'm happy to collect receipt then.
>
> Regards

Whole letter encircled: an issue from the past that throttles the self with fear that others will find out.

11. Retraced letters — how we bind ourselves in chains

A retraced letter is one where the pen travels back over part of the letter. Two letters of the alphabet, the letters 'd' and 't', contain a deliberate retracing of the stem which reinforces the qualities of these movements up into the mountain landscape. However, when retracing occurs in other letters it signifies that the person moves with chains around them, corralled into repeating past patterns and not allowed to set their own goals or frameworks. This action is a trap and the area in which the letter is retraced will tell you where things are caught. In this example below, it is the mountain sweep of the letter 'h' and the valley plunge of the letter 'q' that are retraced and flattened, so this person's inspiration ('h') and emotions ('q') have been squeezed out of them.

Arches occur in the plains landscape of the letters 'h' 'k' 'm' and 'n'. How you write them reflects how you move in and around the structures of your life and how those structures define you and what you wish to achieve. Space between the arches in these letters allows freedom of expression and optimism to flood into a person's life. It is found in the handwriting of people who dare to be different in their thinking and creativity, who have the courage to break away from the rigidity of rules which have been imposed on them by others, and will take risks for greater fulfilment in their life. It is a sign of confidence and independence.

In the examples above, the letter 'm' has been written with retraced downstrokes. Like clenched teeth or a squeezed accordion, or someone hugging themselves tightly, this handwriting ensures that the person's unique creativity is held captive.

In this person's handwriting above the 'm' is written with spaces between the arches, what Vimala Rodgers calls a 'pull away' stroke, as it enables the writer to pull away from the voices and dictates of the past and to shape the present as they want it to be.[5]

---

5. Vimala Rodgers, *Change Your Handwriting, Change Your Life* (Berkeley: Celestial Arts, 1993), p.68.

12. Trigger words — shadows on the grass that reveal our hidden intentions

Handwriting is communication. When we read it we are seeing and sensing much more than the words on the page. However, the words themselves carry meaning and some words we write can provoke an unconscious reaction to an internal process. They are trigger words because they trigger unconscious issues inside us, so the rhythm and shape of the word is influenced by the psychological association the writer has with that particular word.

In the example above, the world 'kind' in the second line is a trigger word. The capital 'K' in the middle of the sentence suggests the invitation is not felt to be 'kind' at all but a burden, as the content of her letter indicates that her life at that time was in some turmoil.

In the example above, the woman writes that she has 'never married' and the space before the word 'married' indicates that this is a trigger word. Even though it might be argued that she is simply avoiding the lower loop of the letter 'f' from the line above, we write at the pace we hear the words. The size of the space reflects her hesitation before she puts pen to paper and implies that she may now unconsciously regret the rebellion of her youth.

The subject, and software In trigued me and I was priveleged enough to afford the time .

In the example above, the space before the word 'intrigued' indicates the writer was searching for the appropriate word to describe the software. It is a trigger word in that it implies the writer had not encountered the ideas and concepts contained in the software, and that his interior world was shifting as a result. On the other hand, the phrase 'afford the time' is written crammed together. Even though the writer notes that he could 'afford the time', the spacing indicates that the time was paid for dearly and he had to make up that time by fitting a lot more into less of his schedule.

have often been described as arrogant, his debating technique being that of attacking his opponents with force,

In the example above, the word 'attacking' is a trigger word. Compare the letter 'g' in the words 'arrogant', 'debating' and 'being' with that of 'attacking'. The writer is describing a politician whom she does not like and she has shaped her letter 'g' like a cobra at the ready, in the same way as she visualizes this politician.

*there is wisedom in you decision
& that it's OK with me .*

In the example above, the words 'with me' are trigger words. They are both written lower than the rest of the sentence and incline downwards. Although the words state that the decision is OK with this woman, the writing tells you it is a pessimistic acceptance of the inevitable.

Finding the Pattern

Pattern-seeking when reading hand-writing in order to understand behaviour follows the same principles as it does for reading natal charts: we look at all the variations and balance them one against the other in order to draw a conclusion, remembering that any variation within a handwriting trait will reflect the ease or difficulty of an issue in the natal chart, and that severe distortion in any area of the handwriting, if it is followed by other distortions, will point to deep-seated inner turmoil somewhere in the natal chart. This chapter has been concerned with the broad brush strokes of a person's handwriting as a way of understanding the playing field, and the patterns of handwriting as a way of approaching the astrology.

Handwriting checklist summary

1. How does it sit on the page? Are there wide or tight margins? Does it begin close to the edges of the pages, left (past), right (future), top (familiarity) or bottom (time management)? This will tell you how you relate to your environment: the way you move on the page is the way you move through life.

2. What is the spacing like between lines and between words? This will tell you how you connect with others, whether you allow new thoughts into your thinking or whether you crowd others with your own thoughts.

3. Is there a predominance of letters within one of the three landscapes? Is there a greater movement in one area than another, or is there a balance between your goals and what inspires you, the practical application of those goals and the emotions and feelings that thread them together?

4. In what direction do your letters slant? Letter slant reveals the compass directions of your life — how you reach out towards or pull away from life.

5. In what direction do your lines of writing slant? Line slant reveals your confidence — what you believe will be the outcome of your ventures.

6. What is the size of your letters? The size of the letters you write are the footprints you make, how you tread upon the earth.

7. How do your letters connect with each other? The way they connect is how you connect with others through your thoughts, feelings and attitudes, and how you find solutions to problems.

8. What sort of pressure do you apply to your life? What is the force of your personality?

9. How do you begin and end words? This is an indication of how you step into, step out of and step on from situations.

10. Do your letters contain any hidden agendas? Are there any issues from which you are unconsciously hiding?

11. Are there any retraced letters in your handwriting? Is there any place where you are moving with chains around you, repeating past patterns and not allowing yourself to set your own goals or frameworks?

12. Does your handwriting contain any trigger words, any shadows on the grass that reveal hidden intentions?

4

The Alphabet - The Shape of Language

We live in a world of colour, sound and information, so we are used to seeing and hearing whole images rather than parts. So when it comes to handwriting we tend to do the same and see whole concepts rather than individual letters. Yet as we have seen in Chapter Three, the way we convey information to ourselves and others through handwriting is a result of the way we specifically shape and link our letters with other letters.

Nearly 4,000 years ago the *Sepher Yetzirah*, the earliest document we have about the way the letters of the alphabet are shaped and formed, acknowledged that the God of the Old Testament created the whole world by inscribing and combining the letters of the alphabet in every possible way.[1] In a manner of speaking God's 'handwriting' created the whole world and in this same way your handwriting creates your world. For just as this great movement of creation comes through combining and shaping the letters of the alphabet, so it is individualized in our personal handwriting. As you connect each individual letter with other letters, so writing becomes your personal pathway to creating your world.

However, whole images are first created by their parts, so the way we fashion individual letters influences the whole. This chapter is concerned with showing you those initial shapes and indicating their meaning.

The Language of Letters

As we shape our letters there are four directions in which our hand moves when we write: clockwise and anticlockwise, away from the body and towards the body; and two directions in which they can complete, to the left and to the right. When we move our pen away from our bodies and up the page we can think of this as us relating to the outer world of ambitions and goals. When we move our pen towards us and our body we can think of this as us relating to our personal world of thoughts, feelings and emotions. Clockwise movements keep us in tune with

---

1. Aryeh Kaplan, *Sefer Yetzirah, the Book of Creation*, Revised Edition (San Francisco: Red Wheel/ Weiser, 1997), p.124.

the rhythms of the regulated world, following the direction in which the hands of a timepiece move, based on the movement of the Sun across the sky in the northern hemisphere. In contrast, anticlockwise movements allow us to access a different time and space, that which we could call 'otherworld' or imaginary or enchanted or meditative time. When letters complete by moving towards the left they draw us back into the past in some way. When letters complete by moving towards the right they allow us to reach out to others and to the future. So there is a language in letters which contains a story:

◈ The letters 'h', 'k', 'l' and 't', if made with a loop moving up the page, sweep away from the body embracing the outer world, showing how we reach for our dreams and ambitions (the sweep up into the mountain part of the landscape). Then we complete the letter by planting this loop into the practical plains landscape of our writing which is the practical area of our life. So these letters are about giving our goals, that which inspires us, an expression and also a practical base.

◈ The letters 'f', 'j', 'p', 'q', 'y' and sometimes 'z', reach down below the line towards our body and so into our emotions. Then we complete the letter by bringing it back up into our mundane world. As a result these letters allow us to give a practical expression to our feelings.

◈ The letters 'b', 'j' and 'p' (and 'z' if written with a lower loop) carry clockwise motion, allowing us to access the rhythms of the regulated world.

◈ The letters 'a', 'c', 'd', 'f', 'l', 'o' and 'q' can all carry an anticlockwise motion, helping us access 'otherworld' time.

◈ The letters 'g', 'k', 's' and 'y' (depending on how they are shaped) carry clockwise and anticlockwise motions, suggesting that they are accessing both types of motion and hence allowing us to experience both types of time — practical as well as 'otherworld'.

◈ The letters 'b', 'o', 'p', 's' and 'x' complete their movements on the left, helping us to review or access the past.

◈ The letters 'a', 'c', 'd', 'e', 'f', 'g', 'h', 'i', 'j', 'k', 'l', 'm', 'n', 'q', 'r', 't', 'u', 'v', 'w', 'y' and 'z' can all complete their movements on the right, allowing us to reach out to others and to the future. Whilst this rightward movement is essential in allowing us to move across the page and create communication that is not continually going back on itself, we can see that our alphabet in the west is biased towards the future. Indeed the differences between cultures and what it means to define the past and the future in terms of the compass directions are graphically depicted in the landscape of handwriting. For those cultures that employ alphabets that are written from right to left, such as the Hebrew and Arabic alphabets, their 'past' is the right hand side of the page and their 'future' is the left. For traditional Chinese, Japanese, and Korean cultures, writing in vertical columns from right to left facilitated writing with a brush in the right hand whilst continually unrolling the sheet of paper or scroll with the left, so the top of the page becomes the 'past' and the bottom of the page the 'future'. This may speak of societies for whom sky (top of the page) and landscape (bottom of the page) had more meaning in terms of past and future rather than the diurnal cycle of sunrise-sunset, left to right, east to west horizontal movement. However, with the implementation of the communist revolution in 1949, the People's Republic of China mandated that horizontal text should be used, and on 1st January 1956 all newspapers in mainland China were changed from vertical to horizontal alignment. This huge cultural change of perspective was thus reflected in the change of direction in the handwriting.

Changing any of these directions will have a profound effect in our life. For example, we are taught to write the letter 'o' in an anticlockwise direction. Turning this around to write it clockwise, changing the course and direction of its flow, can literally turn your world around, changing the course and direction of its expression.

Gesture and thought

Since the 1970s,[2] gestures have come to be regarded as 'parts of *language itself* — not as embellishment or elaborations, but as integral parts of the processes of language and its use.'[3]

As McNeil notes,

> ...language is inseparable from imagery. The imagery in question is embodied in the gestures that universally and automatically occur with speech. Such gestures are a necessary component of speaking and thinking.[4]

Gestures are such active participants in both speaking and thinking that we take them for granted and they become seamless threads of conversation. Yet the observation of any exchange between two or more people illustrates just how

---

2. Adam Kendon, 'Some Relationships between Body Motion and Speech,' in *Studies in Dyadic Communication*, ed. Siegman A. and Pope B. (New York: Pergammon Press, 1972), pp.177-210.
3. David McNeill, *Gesture and Thought* (Chicago: Chicago University Press, 2007), p.13.
4. Ibid, p.15.

much an integral part of conversation gesture has become and the garment of speech would fall apart or appear sterile if gestures were stripped away from it.

We also apply gesture to our written work. We use the shape of the letters to carry meaning and the gestures within them to convey our beliefs, attitudes, approaches, needs, desires and goals, along with our conscious and unconscious history.

How our world becomes manifest

As part of our formal educational process we acquire handwriting by being taught a model of the alphabet and each country, culture and historical period has its own handwriting systems. However, what we produce as a child is often an awkward attempt to imitate copybook forms, so what we are creating is not so much 'handwriting' as artistic representation. It is over these two or three influential years in early childhood, as memory gradually connects form and meaning so we no longer have to copy the shapes, that we introduce our own individual variations or deviations from this initial template. This is the beginning of 'handwriting', and some of the characteristics that come into play that produce our unique handwriting include the way we file images in our brain and the way we retrieve them, our ability to make a replica of those images on the page, our ability to co-ordinate our hand with our eye in forming those images, the way we hold our writing instrument, the way we sit to write, and so on. When these individual traits become routine and we produce handwriting focused on the thought behind the words rather than the movement of the pen, then our handwriting is said to have matured and become our own. As document investigator Frank Harley Norwitch notes, your handwriting is different to the handwriting of any other individual in the world. Like fingerprints, there are no two handwriting styles that are exactly alike.[5]

Perhaps more importantly for understanding AstroGraphology, in the process of creating our own handwriting we often introduce embellishments which we think are pleasing to the eye or take shortcuts to write a letter more rapidly but which have a more profound underlying meaning in their ability to reveal aspects in your natal chart. I was recently asked by a young woman named Jane whether copying another person's handwriting meant that we were taking on their issues, rather than dealing with them. She had noticed that some of her letters held containers and explained the reason for them in her writing as follows:

> I was about nineteen and working with someone who had beautiful flowery writing. She was herself a pretty, bubbly, curly haired sort of person that everyone

5. Norwitch, Frank Harley. Norwitch Document Laboratory. http://www.questioneddocuments.com. (25 January 2009).

loved, and at the time I was a spotty, scrawny end of teens kinda gal! I remember trying the same colour lipstick in an effort to have the magnetism she seemed to possess, and copying her writing because it was so lovely — and she did the loops. I also remember someone that worked with us for a while who told me how she had practised her letter 'r' (which looked amazing) because she had seen it in someone's writing. I liked it, too, and it has definitively affected my writing. So my big question — as you can imagine — is how authentic is our own particular style? When I look back at my school writing, and before I started trying to grow out of the lack of confidence that crucified me in my early years, my writing is clear and uncomplicated with no loops or twirly bits. What does it all mean? Am I unwittingly carrying other peoples' stuff with me? In doing the loops have I unknowingly amassed a pile of secrets and hidden traits? I am absolutely fascinated.

In recognizing more consciously what containers mean in certain letters, Jane revisited her adolescent handwriting, created at a time when she felt herself to be tormented by a lack of confidence. In so doing she describes her handwriting as 'clear and uncomplicated' but given the way she felt, perhaps a better description might be 'facing the elements without protection'. In seeking a better role model for herself, Jane then copied some of the traits she saw in the handwriting of someone she deemed popular in order to obtain the qualities the popular young woman displayed. Teenagers do this constantly, imitating a walk, a style of dress, a haircut or a stance of their personal heroes, believing it will empower them in the same way. Jane might just as easily have copied the popular woman's body stance or voice patterns but she chose to protect some of her awkward painful characteristics in containers on the left of some of her letters until she was able to look at them more readily when older.

Knowing Jane has a Moon-Neptune aspect in her chart helps to understand the reasons why she did so. Such a configuration suggests the instinctive ability to merge emotionally with another. However, it also translates into a susceptibility to the emotional environment around the person, and such a person will often find themselves unconsciously doing what pleases other people instead of what pleases them. When flooded with the sea of many people's emotions, feeling infringed and intruded upon can prove unnerving, translating into a lack of confidence. Thus the person will seek ways of shielding and protecting themselves against this emotional barrage, even becoming someone else as a form of escape from these overwhelming situations. In Jane's case the containers on the left provided a safe-haven for her feelings of inadequacy and lack of confidence, a physical reassurance every time she wrote that this part of her psyche was handling the pain for her. This is neither to be condemned nor condoned, simply to be understood so that better choices can be made in the future.

Since handwriting contains a language and a story, many issues with which people struggle are often apparent in just one of the words they write. As a way of helping you see this, I have gathered together examples of these in an Addendum called 'A Guide to the Living Alphabet', at the end of the book. Later in the book I will look at whole pages of writing and correlate them with natal charts. Meanwhile what follows are the more obviously difficult gestures that can become embedded into certain single letters. Look to see if your handwriting contains any of these.

c

The letter 'c' is one letter that can contain hooks. There are many types of hooks from softly-rounded coat hooks to barbed fish hooks. The point of a hook is to hold or hang on to something. With a fish-hook, the barb influences how strongly the

hook can hold on, so when there is a fish hook in the letter 'c' it reveals someone who is impaled by their own past, someone who is holding onto or held by buried negative experiences which, since it occurs in the plains landscape, influences the person's practical world. The degree of complexity of the hook denotes the degree to which the person uses malice and hostility themselves or feels used by the cruelty of others.

d

An inflated letter 'd' stem is a storage container for an accumulation of blame and self-sabotage. The more exaggerated the loop, the more it can resemble a heavy 'backpack' of emotions which collects and festers. Inflated 'd' stems can be found in the handwriting of those who blame others for their difficulties, yet are fearful of confrontation and defining clear boundaries about what they will and won't undertake and what they emotionally need or want. These are people who will interpret what is being said rather than understand it and can easily mistranslate comments and take them personally. Often called a Cleopatra loop because it graphically represents the 'Queen of Denial',[6] this can also turn into a Santa Claus loop when it becomes grossly distended, as in the third example below. Here the small initial circle describing the ego's sense of wholeness in the

---

6.   Vimala Rodgers, *Change Your Handwriting, Change Your Life* (Berkeley: Celestial Arts, 1993), p.104.

practical world suffers under the burden of taking on everyone else's problems rather than attending to their own, and any personal talent or creativity is suppressed or denied.

f

The letter 'f' is the only letter which covers all three landscapes and as such maintains a unique position in the alphabet. Shaped as a 'bow-and-arrow', moving into the mountain landscape with a full loop, travelling down in a vertical line into the valley landscape and forming a lower loop which then returns to meet the mountain loop in the centre before moving off to the right, it has the ability to give us balance.

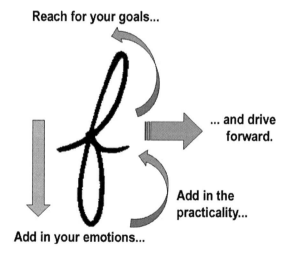

When it is shaped as a 'propeller f' it becomes another self-sabotage movement. The person reaches for their goals and dreams with the sweeping movement up into their mountain landscape away from the body and then reverses the flow of energy via a counter move in their valley landscape towards the body. Making propeller shapes on a page in this way is excellent for calming oneself in a tense

situation, as this movement is the same as treading water, expending energy but going nowhere. It is often found in the handwriting of people who are in a double bind about success in any context. Such people long for the acclaim and respect that success brings but are unconsciously blocked by profound fears and therefore sabotage themselves at the last moment.

I — First person singular

The personal pronoun 'I' meaning 'self' is a particular case of a capital letter. We could say that it correlates with the meaning for the Sun — our sense of ego, identity and vitality — so how we write this is profound. A small 'I' suggests a feeling of inferiority, a large 'I', suggests superiority, and an over-inflated 'I' suggests bluff. An 'I' slanting to the left implies seclusion and being drawn to the past, as does an 'I' written close to the preceding word. An 'I' slanting to the right signals being drawn to the future. An upright 'I' as well as an 'I' with even spaces on either side of it indicates independence and being able to stand in the world with confidence. An 'I' that varies in size or direction indicates oscillation in the person's ego, identity and vitality. An 'I' written with serifs, lines above and below the letter, places boundaries around itself, yet also offers strength and confidence. For someone who feels adrift in the world, changing their capital 'I' to one like this can anchor and ground them. For someone who has been writing their capital letter 'I' with serifs, removing them can be a release from ceilings they have placed upon themselves.

Changing your 'I's can literally 'change your eyes' as to how you see yourself placed in the world.

'i' dots

A common saying for many of us is to make sure that we dot our 'i's and cross our 't's. What we mean by this is to make sure that we have attended to the fine details of our life. The dot above the 'i' is called a superscript dot and was added to the letter in the Middle Ages so it could be distinguished from the letters 'u', 'm' and 'n' if they were written next to it, as they also incorporate vertical strokes. 'j' is a variant form of 'i' which also emerged at this time and later became a separate letter. Thus the superscript dot is a distinguisher that adds clarity.

An 'i' dot placed directly above the 'i' indicates someone who is present in how they think, speculate, hope and plan. They pay attention to detail and therefore have good powers of concentration.

If the 'i' dot is placed too high overhead, however, the person may feel that what they want to achieve is literally out of reach, too far up the mountain to obtain.

An 'i' dot placed to the left of the letter indicates someone who lacks self-confidence by being trapped by plans and dreams from the past and thus becomes withdrawn, or else trapped by relationship issues which have not yet been resolved.

An 'i' dot placed to the right of the letter indicates someone who is future-orientated, enthusiastic and often impulsive. However, they may also be so caught in the hopes of what might occur that they haven't yet put their ideas into place.

When an 'i' dot gets missed altogether, this indicates someone who is careless of detail or scattered in their thinking. In this example, where the person has written the world 'ability', the person has also omitted to cross their letter 't'.

'i' dots can also express anger and resentment in the form of a slash, a stab, a jag or a hook:

An 'i' dot made as a half circle open on the right is often called the 'watching eye' and designates observation.

(Living) 'i' dots can also express creativity when they link to another part of the word.

An 'i' dot made as a full circle is a call for attention, often found in the writing of young or adolescent girls, where it suggests creative ability but with a lack of direction, someone who holds onto dreams and plans that they do not feel capable of manifesting. It can be found in the handwriting of artists and designers as a way of expressing uniqueness. However it is also a container and therefore indicates someone who is hiding or concealing something, and may signify someone who wishes to project an image of sophistication and culture. In this case as it is close to the 'i' stem, what they are concealing exists in the practical areas of this person's life.

't' bars

Many of us are taught that a capital T must be crossed at the top but that when we write a small 't' we must place the cross bar lower down the vertical stem. Like the letters 'b' and 'd', the vertical stem of a small 't' extends from the plains into the mountains of our lives. Yet the small 't' is unique in that it is the only letter with a cross-bar. This cross bar is moveable; how high you place this cross bar tells you how high you are willing to reach up in order to accomplish your goals. The 't' stem and its cross-bar therefore becomes a tool for helping us to blend the region of practicality, the plains of our life, with the mountains to activate our dreaming and make it manifest. Thus it becomes a letter connected with our belief in ourselves and our abilities. Have a look at where you have placed the cross-bar of your 't' and if you are having difficulty bringing your plans into realization, raise the cross-bar to the top, making sure it is written firmly on equal sides of the stem and drawn slightly tilted from lower left to upper right.

In workshops I have often been surprised by students who look at me and say 'But you can't do that. It's against the rules'. 'Whose rules?' I ask?

Reach up towards your goals...

... then optimistically place how how you intend to achieve with your life.

... reinforce them in the practical area...

The 't' stem also represents time - beginnings and endings - so when the bar appears only to the left of the stem it indicates some area of resistance connected with goals and the future (on the right).

A cross-bar on the left of the vertical stem and touching it indicates someone who begins well but cannot complete, fearing social contact and being held by the past.

When this is emphasized with the half-bowl on the left, it suggests they are holding onto burdensome issues from the past.

A cross-bar on the left of the vertical stem but not touching it indicates someone who either puts things off until the last minute or is indecisive and strongly influenced by past events.

When the cross-bar appears only to the right of the stem, it represents some area of resistance on the left, suggesting that the writer has difficulty initiating or beginning projects.

A cross-bar on the right of the vertical stem and touching it indicates someone is good at completing, thus prefers to work as part of a team where they are not responsible for initiating projects.

This cross-bar is also on the right of the stem, but rising; this is someone who complete projects with optimism.

A rising cross-bar on the right of the vertical stem but not touching it indicates someone with ambition but little stamina and persistence to achieve what they want.

A falling cross-bar on the right of the vertical stem and not touching it indicates a lack of persistence. It may also indicate the person has become depressed as a result of their lack of achievement.

A cross-bar that slopes downwards from top left to bottom right indicates someone who needs to be in control.

A cross-bar rising and across both sides high but detached suggests someone with ambition and persistence but whose goals are unrealistic.

 A cross-bar that contains a hook indicates someone whose ambition is thwarted by issues which hook them back into the past.

 This letter 't' is crossed back on itself and ends with a hook, indicating that this person has experienced disappointments in life and these issues from the past still tug at them.

 This letter 't' is written with a balloon stem that begins in their mountain landscape. The person is attempting to pull their dreams down into their practical world without laying solid foundations on which they can develop. With nowhere to go, trapped in the container of the 't' stem, these dreams become stagnant.

 No cross bar at all indicates someone who seldom completes what they set out to do, resulting in an underlying feeling of dissatisfaction with life.

Two letters of creativity

I have until now been considering letters which can contain shapes which indicate problematic behaviour. The following two letters are also prone to carrying such traits, but they can also express an inherent creativity.

e

The letter 'e' is often called the letter of the listening ear and it is generally taught in schools to be written like a small letter 'l' thus:

When written as a soft round arc in this way it indicates someone who is a good listener with a high level of patience and empathy. The level of fullness with which the arc is shaped points to the level of the writer's ability to listen. Thus a fully closed arc, here seen in the letter 'e' of 'horoscope', suggests the person is closed to other people's perspectives and ideas.

If there are other factors elsewhere in the writing (a left lean, 't' cross-bars that slope downwards from top left to bottom right, tight and cramped letters), then it may designate a closed mind of a more habitual nature.

In this example below, the second letter 'e' of 'experienced' is closed. Interestingly the sentence in which the word 'experienced' appeared was, "I remember the anguish I experienced..." hence it is understandable that the writer wanted to close herself off from that memory.

experienced

When the letter 'e' is printed, as in the example below, it suggests a desire to be stay within the bounds of one's usual habits and customs. Following rules in this way may mean the person is judgemental when they are presented with new ideas or beliefs. It may also indicate a degree of naivety.

emigrating

Closed 'e' arcs and printed 'e's can be softened by changing them to rounded arcs, leading to greater tolerance of others. This friendly welcoming gesture creates the space where a person can hear other people's ideas without criticism which, in turn, can help a person to think more clearly and respond more imaginatively to life.

An alternative is that it can be formed like a reverse 3. Whether written as a small or capital letter, this is known as a Greek 'e' and is the mark of someone with an agile and responsive mind, someone with fine taste who is well read and seeks cultural input via travel, academic learning, or connecting with other philosophies. With such input, a person's ingenuity can flow more freely.

Ɛ   *Euphoria*

If your writing shows a cramped rigidity and a fear of stepping forward into a more satisfying lifestyle, consider replacing your letter 'e' with a Greek 'e'.

g

The letter 'g' is generally taught in schools to be written as a letter 'a' in the practical plains followed by a sweep down into the valley landscape to embrace our emotions, carrying these back up to be used constructively in our workaday lives and then moving forward to the right (the future), as in the example below.

challenge

In this example the dive into the valley landscape is overemphasized, producing an excess of emotions.

Regards

However, the letter 'g' can also be written like a figure 8. Shaped this way it becomes the mark of a highly fluid, creative and original thinker, someone who can move between different paradigms of thinking and establish their own distinctive position as a result. Thus it is also an indication of someone who brings uniqueness into their profession and sees it as a reflection of who they are, their life purpose, not just a job.

8   Delighted

By shaping the letter 'g' in this way, making sure that the dive into the valley landscape sweeps back up into the practical plains landscape, you can develop your intuition and bring more personal resourcefulness to bear in your life.

If your writing shows inflexibility and a fear of proclaiming your own originality, consider replacing your letter 'g' with a figure-8 'g'.

What do you want to change?

In looking at your own handwriting, as you come to understand what the letters are saying on these deeper levels and where this is reflected in your natal chart, you may decide to make changes to help improve those issues. If you do, you may initially want to shape those letters in a basic form until you can resolve those matters for yourself and create the letter shape in the style you wish, with conscious understanding. For that reason, what I present here is a way to write the letters without difficult gestures embedded into them. Please remember that it will feel strange at first but when you find a part of a letter difficult to write, think about where it falls in its landscape, how it connects with other letters, and what it says about that with which you are currently struggling in your life. As you write, take note of what happens inside you. Where do you feel it in your body? What do you hear being said to you? As you resist shaping part of a letter, what does this say about what you are resisting in your life?

On a clean sheet of paper, play with writing the letters you wish to change.

5

The Chart in the Handwriting

Working with a natal chart is like working with a symphony orchestra. The music originally created in the composer's head can only come to life when the parts written for each individual instrument are played in harmony with each other. Likewise in astrology, we can see the score that the different instruments of the chart are meant to be playing and hear how the 'symphony' is supposed to sound. However, until we sit in consultation with a client, it's hard to know which part of their orchestra is out of tune with the rest.

Handwriting in conjunction with the natal chart offers us the chance to accurately pinpoint in advance which part of the chart is in most need of attention when a client comes to see us. It acts like a fast-track to the client's current issue, bringing it into focus. Instead of spending time on areas that may not need such consideration, the astrologer can zero in more quickly to the issues that are crying out for help.

This technique of correlating handwriting with the issues and themes of the chart works best if you begin slowly, using what you know already to build a picture. So let me introduce you to some people, their handwriting, and their charts.

Please note, I use Ptolemeic, non-cross-sign aspects and the following orbs: conjunction, square, trine and opposition 9 degrees; sextile 4 degrees.

Meet 'Suzanne'...

DOB: 6th November 1964.

Place: Glenelg . South Australia.

Time: 6.50 am

Please send my horoscope with moon sign. Thankyou

Even though this is a small scrap of handwriting, it reveals much about its owner, her thoughts and feelings, and how she sees herself in the world. More importantly it reveals issues that might be relevant for discussion in the consultation room. So what is she presenting to me here? Firstly, Suzanne has offered two sets of handwriting: she has printed her birth data with an even hand and with consistent spaces between the words. However, the request for her horoscope is written in cursive script with the letters tightly bunched together. The printed letters of the birth data are of even height, sit uniformly on a horizontal plane and there is plenty of space between the lines. The cursive letters, however, slope upwards, emphasized in the final signoff, 'Thankyou' written as one word, and the line spacing is tighter. The left hand margin of the printed letters is evenly vertical; the left hand margin of the cursive script moves to the right. Already we can see that there are two opposing sides to this person, the one of the primary school printed letters and the other of the adult cursive script.

Whilst there is a balance of letters in all three landscapes of her life, the eye is drawn to the backward flick of the capital 'P', the backward hooks of the 'y' and 'g', the forward hook on the end of the 'p' of 'horoscope' and the convoluted flourish of the 'y' of 'Thankyou'. These hooks sit below the line in the realm of her emotions. Angles and hooks in the emotional landscape of the valleys are an awkward mix. The leftward movement indicates issues from the past holding her back. If these are family concerns or unresolved emotional issues, they will probably be reflected in her chart by planets or luminaries in the 12th house, or conjunct the South Node, and, being a hook, perhaps planets concerned with betrayal and deception. Even the hook on the 'y' of 'Thankyou', the word itself slanted upwards indicating optimism, moves forward only to be pulled backwards again. As well, tight letters pulled in close point towards fearfulness. Suzanne is not allowing anyone in to her personal space.

This piece of art describes Suzanne's state of mind at the time she requested her horoscope. When she writes her birth data, she uses her intellect; when she makes the request, she is fearful and closed. Already Suzanne has told me a great deal about herself through her handwriting regarding the issues she unconsciously needs to be discussed in an astrological consultation.

Now look at her chart...

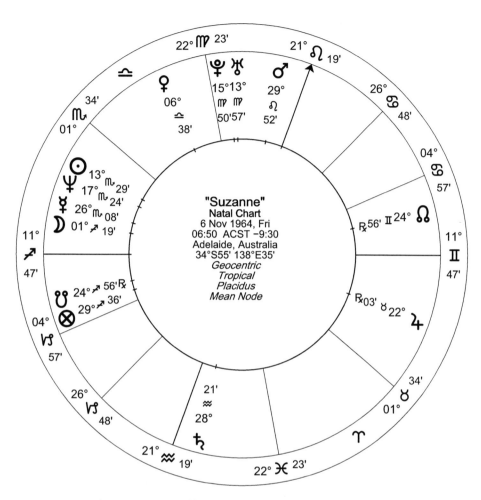

"Suzanne"
Natal Chart
6 Nov 1964, Fri
06:50 ACST −9:30
Adelaide, Australia
34°S55' 138°E35'
Geocentric
Tropical
Placidus
Mean Node

Suzanne was born in 1964 and has a Sagittarian Ascendant. She is seen by others as inspiring and passionate. Her primary drive is to gain power and freedom of action (Fire Ascendant), achieved through the ruler, Jupiter in the 6th house in Taurus square to the MC, making it a pro-active planet. Yet Jupiter is also part of a Fixed Grand Cross.

As astrologers we can observe such a chart and note possible difficulties, the 'netivot' that she may be encountering in this lifetime. The Grand Cross can lay itself open to being too scattered and Suzanne may be running around in circles for other people and not achieving anything of substance for herself. Mars-Saturn can bring in health difficulties, such as arthritis and rheumatism, from issues to do with blocked anger. Unaspected Venus in rulership in the 11th house, ruling the 6th and Libra intercepted in the 11th house, can manifest as her being socially gregarious or feeling inadequate with her ability to connect with others. Likewise

the unaspected Moon in Sagittarius in the 12th house ruling the 8th house, with its deep emotional link to mother who teaches her how to be independent, vacillates between feeling emotionally connected and inspired by change or emotionally disconnected and in upheaval.

However, none of those aspects are making the astrological appointment. Suzanne's handwriting tells you it is the Sun-Neptune-Mercury in Scorpio in the 12th house that has put pen to paper. Suzanne's family issues of betrayal and deception are intense, so much so that she may not even be aware of them, yet Suzanne's handwriting tells you they are dominant issues for her.

What if she consciously changed the hooks to loops? Would this not become a deliberate signal for her every time she made those strokes not to buy into the family pattern, not to repeat the same issues embedded in her family's history? Would this not be a tiny change that could ricochet through her entire life? She could then make more informed choices about how she could explore her Sun-Neptune-Mercury, giving voice to those issues through such avenues as the arts or healing, via some large organization.

A client's handwriting thus becomes an immensely valuable tool in alerting you, as the consulting astrologer, to the Achilles' heel that is ready to change once they have become aware of the issues. For Suzanne, changing the hooks to loops is a way to help her to become conscious of what she is changing in her life every time she writes.

Now meet 'Cheryl'...

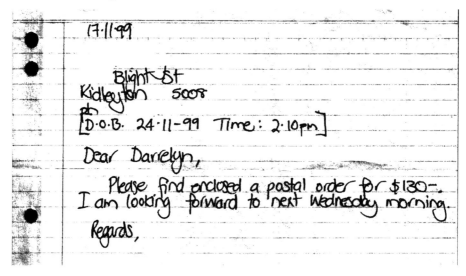

In the handwriting of Cheryl, a young woman born in 1971, the letters are relatively upright, showing clear thinking and objectivity. There is little space between the letters, suggesting the need for close contact or unconscious 'self-hugging', so the writing seems fenced in or bound in some way, suggesting Saturn may be an inhibiting factor in her chart. This is emphasized by the fact that the writing is printed and sits neatly within and on the lines, implying that she 'toes the line' in her life. It can also mean that she needs a crutch to lean on and prefers to follow orders, lacking the confidence to make her own decisions. Additionally the spaces between the words are uneven. Where the uneven spaces come will tell where she hesitates in moving ahead on her 'netivot', suggesting trigger words that cause her nervousness, such as the relatively longer spaces before my name (bowing respectfully to authority) and before the word 'forward'.

Cheryl was coming to see me for a consultation on her birthday the week after she wrote the note, yet she has written the date of her birth as '1999'. Clearly this has influenced her. Unconscious slips like this happen even to the most conscientious of us. It does, however, suggest that time is on her mind, pointing again to Saturn and the fact that she was coming to see me on her twenty-eighth birthday. The correspondence was written on a piece of lined student note paper with punched holes along the side, so perhaps she also wanted to demonstrate to me that she was a student of life, possibly indicating an emphasized third house-ninth house axis in her chart. Her handwriting has no hidden containers but there is a tendency for the tails of the 'f' and 'g' to crash into the line below, suggesting her thoughts are sometimes flooded by her feelings. With few parts of her letters pushing in to the mountains of her dreams, and 't' bars crossed in the practical plains landscape, this is someone with few goals for herself.

Who was I expecting to meet? Who had made the appointment?

Look at her chart...
Cheryl's Sun is in Sagittarius conjunct Neptune in the 9th house in opposition to Saturn in the 3rd house. Her handwriting revealed a good deal regarding her Sun opposition Saturn, the fear of failure reflected in the tightly-held letters. It also reflected her Moon in Aquarius trine Uranus that found emotions so uncomfortable, and her fear of relating embodied by Pluto in the 7th house, causing the letters to bunch up — offering little space for anyone to come into her life. However, where was the artistry and intuition of the Sun conjunct Neptune or her Pisces Ascendant? Where was the fire and passion of all that Sagittarian energy? Where was the ambition of the Jupiter in rulership in the 9th house conjunct the MC and ruler of the Ascendant, or the Mercury-Venus conjunction in Sagittarius in the 10th house also conjunct the MC?

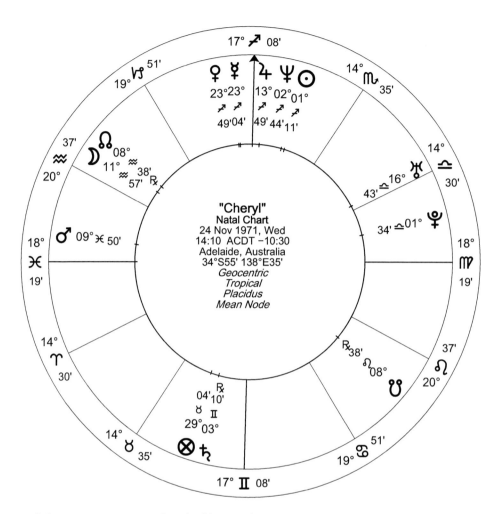

"Cheryl"
Natal Chart
24 Nov 1971, Wed
14:10 ACDT −10:30
Adelaide, Australia
34°S55' 138°E35'
Geocentric
Tropical
Placidus
Mean Node

With her Saturn Return ahead of her and transiting Pluto about to conjunct her MC in 2002, bringing irrevocable change into her social status or career through relationship upheaval, there was much to discuss regarding her fear of being swamped by emotion and passion (Moon in Aquarius in the 11th house conjunct the North Node and trine Uranus). One way of helping her was to suggest she open out her letters to let other people in to her life. At the same time she could make an inventory of what she had already achieved in the world and then create a 'wish list' of her own goals and dreams (Sun-Saturn). To help her reach for these and make them a reality, she could add sweeps up into the mountain landscape of her 'f's and 'l's. Acting as a visual cue every time she made one of these new strokes, the deliberateness of this act would enable her to process and consciously acknowledge some of the changes she wanted to bring into her life. This way, instead of using her Saturn as a shield to hide her confusion (Saturn as the singleton in her chart was also the handle of the bucket of planets held within the five signs stretching between Libra and Pisces), she could begin to redefine herself (Sun-Saturn) as an artist or a healer (Sun-Neptune), as well as a motivated and inspirational teacher (Jupiter conjunct the MC square Mars) with a passion for communication (Venus-Mercury in Sagittarius in the 10th house).

Now meet 'Arthur'...

Arthur's use of printed capital letters in his handwriting shows a tight control of his world. The letters are made with a heavy pressure indicating energy, activity, and, at times, aggression. They also slope towards the right, showing that he reaches out to his future. He even writes that he hopes he will be heading in the 'right' direction in the New Year. There is adequate space between the letters, words and lines, showing clarity of thought, organizing ability, and a balanced perspective. However, his handwriting is boxed firmly within the narrow parallel tramlines of his mundane world, allowing few emotions to escape. Arthur's handwriting shows two needs: the right slope and the letter-word space shows that he wants to move ahead in his life and that he has the organizational ability to do so; however, the use of capital letters shows great fear of doing so. This is the handwriting of someone trapped in a world that has become a prison.

Look at his chart…

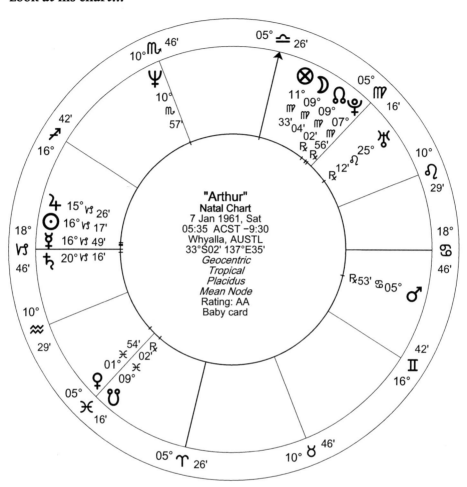

"Arthur"
Natal Chart
7 Jan 1961, Sat
05:35 ACST −9:30
Whyalla, AUSTL
33°S02' 137°E35'
Geocentric
Tropical
Placidus
Mean Node
Rating: AA
Baby card

Arthur was born in 1961. When he came to see me in late 2001 he was employed as a financial advisor for a large investment company. His words were that he 'gets up every day hating to go in to work'. He also played the stock market. In his consultation he wanted to know about his personal finances and wealth. He admitted that he was a gambler, preferring to rush passionately forward and turn money around in a day. However, he had lost a great deal of money through the fall of the Australian dollar after the terrorist attack in the USA (9/11) so his finances were (he said) in a volatile situation. What he really wanted to do was to set up as an independent consultant but he was extremely fearful of failure and what his friends would think. Romance and love were also difficult areas in his life. Arthur was attracted to empowered, critical women and these relationships continually ended explosively.

The stellium in Capricorn on the Ascendant contains issues of fear of failure and inadequacy (Sun-Saturn and Saturn in rulership), role-modelled by enterprises of both father and grandfather which may have gone awry (Sun-Jupiter with the Sun ruling the 8th house and Jupiter ruling the 12th house and in fall). It also contains issues of inhibited communication or feeling mentally inferior (Mercury conjunct Saturn, with Saturn in rulership and Mercury in the degree of the Sun and in 'the other place' with the Sun).[1]

Having an earth Ascendant emphasizes Arthur's need for physical security, reinforced by having the ruler of the Ascendant (Saturn) conjunct the Ascendant and in rulership. Arthur wants to be seen as responsible and he needs physical security in order to do so. It is fair to suggest that Saturn is 'in charge' of the stellium, valiantly attempting to shore up Arthur's feelings of inadequacy (Sun-Saturn) and mental inferiority (Mercury-Saturn) by over-control. This was the trap Arthur set up for himself: he wanted to take a risk by stepping out of his well-paid job and position himself as an independent financial consultant. However, feeling inadequate to rise to the level of expectation set by his father-figure (Sun-Saturn), he feared failure and feared repeating the actions of his grandfather (Jupiter in fall in the 12th house ruling the 12th house). To relieve the pressure of the stellium, Arthur's Jupiter took risks with gambling instead.

At my suggestion in the consultation, Arthur began to use cursive writing rather than capitals to help understand his fear of failure. In so doing, he set in train a whole avenue of exploration of other parts of his chart, in particular his Venus in Pisces conjunct the South Node and the Venus-Mars-Neptune water Grand Trine. Every time he wrote rather than printed he gave himself a clear signal of his willingness to surrender more to his intuition which in turn began to inform him on how to handle money better (Venus-Pluto), instead of feeling betrayed by monetary transactions. As he gained confidence from this approach so he gained confidence in other areas of his life, such as further study (3rd house-9th house axis). This then allowed him to channel his obsessive tendencies (Moon in Virgo conjunct Pluto), into something positive rather than them finding a difficult expression in his personal relationships. Armed with an academic imprimatur he was then able to step into the business world as a consultant and sole trader, responsible for his own failures but now better understanding how they formed

---

1. In visual astrology Mercury would be invisible when it is this close to the Sun, and therefore travelling with the Sun into the underworld after sunset and remaining invisible for the whole of the night. This phenomenon of obscurity when a planet is swallowed up in the light of the Sun has been termed 'combustion' and a planet is said to be devoid of its strength when in combustion or combust. However, in empirical work with clients I have found that this is not always the case. It often appears to take on a more alternative flavour, in this case, being Mercury, thinking differently to others.

one of his pathways ('netivot') towards achieving success. As he gained business qualifications so he began to lecture and teach and found that instead of helplessly forming relationships with commanding, critical women (Moon conjunct Pluto in Virgo), he became self-empowered and could use discernment (Venus in Pisces) when it came to relating.

Arthur's handwriting revealed which part of his chart was in charge at the time that he came to see me and therefore gave a clear direction as to how that part could be assisted.

Now meet 'Catherine' ...

13.7.99

Darrelyn,

I have enclosed a cheque as a deposit for appointment on Tuesday 3rd August 1999, @ 10.00 am.

I have also checked Michaels birth time - it was 13:34 on 3rd January 1999.

Looking forward to seeing you ~

Catherine's handwritten note reveals an ambivalence in how she approaches and interacts with the world. There is good organization of space between the words and lines in general, showing orderliness, the ability to think and speak clearly and plan her life economically. As well, the letters sit mostly in the plains landscape, indicating a practical approach to life. However, the narrow margin hugging the left side of the page indicates fear of the future, someone who does not seek personal contact, pointing to the possibility of a luminary in Pisces or the 12th house. Adding to this are her evenly-shaped but tightly cramped letters representative of the need for close contact or unconscious 'self-hugging'. There is a mix of letters that lean to the left and those that sit upright, reinforcing this internal conflict.

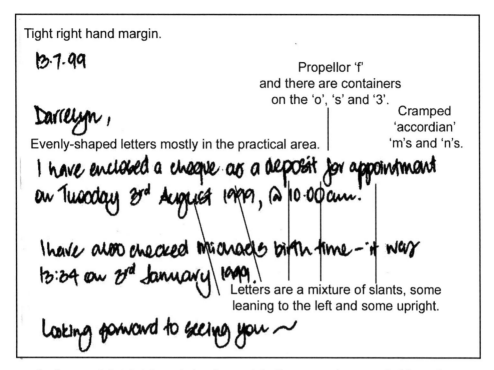

Tight right hand margin.

13.7.99

Propellor 'f'
and there are containers
on the 'o', 's' and '3'.

Cramped
'accordian'
'm's and 'n's.

Darrelyn,

Evenly-shaped letters mostly in the practical area.

I have enclosed a cheque as a deposit for appointment on Tuesday 3rd August 1999, @ 10.00am.

I have also checked Michaels birth time – it was 13:34 on 3rd January 1999.

Letters are a mixture of slants, some leaning to the left and some upright.

Looking forward to seeing you ~

The letters 'o', 'p', 's', and the figure '3' all contain luggage holds and since these occur as she makes a movement forward to the future, it suggests she is preoccupied with information she is holding about others in confidence or through accident which she cannot disclose. There is a further container in the 'd' of 'checked', this time on the left hand side, suggesting she is holding onto something from the past or else shielding or protecting something about herself.

To add to the story, she uses two types of 'f'. One is the propeller 'f', the 'f' of fear of success, of someone who subtly sabotages themselves at the last moment; the other with a lower loop only is the 'f' of the person who brings other people's plans to fruition rather than their own. Indeed Catherine's handwriting shows almost no desire to venture into her mountain landscape and formulate her own goals or dreams. The cross bar of the 't' drawn evenly from left to right and moving slightly upwards, indicative of optimism, still sits low in the plains landscape. The nets into her valleys and her emotions through the lower loops of the letters 'g' and 'y' are closed when they begin a word or occur in the middle but open when they end it (she is pulled back to her past as she completes matters), suggesting an inconsistency of emotions.

Finally her personal pronoun 'I' is a stick only, suggesting on the one hand straightforwardness, openness and a wish to be seen as she is; on the other hand, however, its lean to the left and its proximity to 'have' the second time this phrase

'I have' is written suggest a growing anxiety, feelings of inferiority and a plea for withdrawal, pointing to the possibility of a lack of Fire, or else Mars in detriment or fall or hidden in the 12th house or conjunct the South Node.

What part of her chart is coming to the consultation?

Look at her chart ...

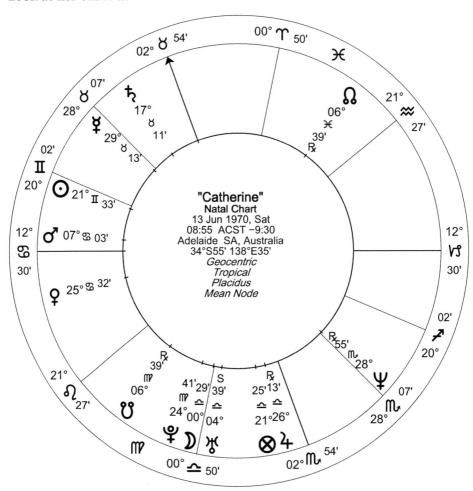

Catherine was born in 1970 and came to see me in 1999. Her Cancer Ascendant, along with Mars in Cancer in the 12th house and conjunct it, made sense of her need for emotional security revealed in her handwriting. As well, the ruler of that Ascendant, Moon in Libra conjunct Uranus, indicating the striving for emotional independence through ideas, debate and consensus, clarified why her handwriting was focused into the practical plains area. However, the underlying dissonance of Mars in Cancer square Moon-Uranus was a concern.

This aspect in Catherine's chart suggests a fast or sudden birth (Mars-Uranus) where cutting is involved (Moon-Mars), or else that she had fever as a baby (Moon-Mars) and hence was unable to be reassured by mother on a body level (Moon-Uranus). Even though mother is trying to keep things in balance (Moon in Libra), the astrology is suggesting that she is experienced by Catherine as emotionally detached (Moon-Uranus).

There is another anomaly within this aspect, for whilst it describes someone with fast, physical energy and a high libido (Mars-Uranus), Catherine prefers to take action when it feels right (Mars in Cancer) and in order for this to happen, she has to be emotionally confident that all parties are in harmony (Moon in Libra). This difficult juggling act can lead to accumulated resentment and bitterness, seen in Catherine's handwriting as the luggage holds of her 'd', 'o', 'p', 's', and the figure '3'.

Added to the story is her weakened, absent or mythic father figure (Sun in the 12th house) who is not around to show her how to initiate and take action in the world (Sun-Pluto). As a consequence there is reticence in engaging with the world, since she has learnt at a young age that following the masculine model for doing so will let her down. This is seen in the leftward slant of her letters, the close proximity of her handwriting to the left hand margin, and the concertina effect. Furthermore her low-crossed 't' bars show no ambition or personal goal setting, despite an unaspected Saturn in the 10th house ruling both the 7th and 8th houses. This, it would seem, had been projected onto her husband. Indeed in classic expression of her Saturn Return, Catherine had given birth to her second child (her first son) seven months earlier. Now she organized her schedule and timetables around the two children and her husband, who worked in a managerial position for a car manufacturing company.

Finally, nothing in her handwriting revealed her creativity (Mercury in Taurus opposition Neptune across the 5th-11th axis, Neptune-Venus Water trine), her gift of imagination (Mercury-Neptune, Venus-Neptune) and her ability to bed that into fertile soil (Mercury in Taurus).

There were several ways to help Catherine begin to realize the potential of her 'netivot'. The easiest way to set that journey in motion was to get her to move the left hand margin of her handwriting slightly closer to the right, gently releasing herself from the hold of her past. At the same time, bearing in mind that she had two small children in her care, she could begin a home-based fitness programme using weights (Mars in Cancer square Uranus). Reasoning that she had to be healthy to look after her family, this not only helped her to acquire strength and energy but allowed her to set practical goals for herself (Saturn in the 10th house). In doing so she learned to achieve personal goals in small incremental steps

(Sun-Pluto) and at the same time learned to trust her body (Moon-Mars-Uranus). As she engaged with this process, she could then bring in other changes to her handwriting, lifting the t-bar, expanding the letters and changing the propeller 'f' to a bow-and-arrow 'f'. Using the 'excuse' of her children, Catherine began creating stories and then writing them down, and for the first time experienced the joy of creative expression.

None of this happened overnight and as Catherine moved forward with the changes, many unresolved issues percolated to the surface and forced her to look at them in the clear light of day. However, using this technique she was able to identify old patterns and begin the process of changing them or releasing them, watching her handwriting as the marker for how she was exploring and co-creating her future.

Now look at Margaret Thatcher, the first woman British Prime Minister ...

Margaret Thatcher's handwriting has an upward slant, signifying an optimistic approach to her world. The writing maintains an even baseline, showing an ability to plan ahead and, as this is coupled with small writing, she has excellent powers of concentration and an aptitude for detail. There is also a generous amount of space between each word and between the lines, indicating someone who welcomes other people's ideas, as well as a private person who can put space and solitude around herself when necessary.

Nevertheless there are also several features which indicate areas of insecurity. Firstly, the relatively small capital 'I' pronoun suggests that, despite the air of authority, a part of her still feels intimidated by the position she holds. Secondly, the high bar of he letter 't' indicates lofty ambitions and when the stroke is long, forceful and to the right of the stem it suggests an ability to complete what others start. However, the t-bars are much higher than other letters of a comparable height such as 'd', 'k' or 'f' and often the bars do not touch the stem. This is someone who either sets unreachable goals or is never satisfied with what she does achieve. Furthermore she may bite off more than she can chew and then become upset or frustrated when she cannot complete matters. Her capital 'M' is written in the same way as she writes her capital 'th' of 'Thank you' and 'Thatcher', and being larger than her surname, indicates that she regards herself as more important than her family. Yet in shape this looks like a cape and, being the initial letter of her first name, suggests that she protects herself from others. Her letter 'g' is highly creative. However, the propeller 'f' implies that she moves forward in her life only to sabotage or jeopardize her actions in some way.

Now let's look at her chart...

Margaret Thatcher's tenacity and ambition can be seen in her Saturn conjunct the Ascendant and, being connected with the 3rd house by rulership and interception, it gave her the voice of authority. Nevertheless Saturn conjunct the Ascendant indicates an inferiority complex that she hides from public view yet which sits in her handwriting as the small capital 'I' pronoun. Hence she works harder and longer than other people as a way of hiding this fear of failure (the unanchored t-bars).

This drive for knowledge as a source of power is embodied in the cardinal T-square (Mars-Pluto-Jupiter) and yet with Jupiter in fall and Mars in detriment she was being asked to employ alternative, non-mainstream ways of solving problems when it came to resources and groups. This was not her way and the propeller 'f' in her handwriting, the small capital 'I' and the unanchored t-bars are windows into her vulnerabilities.

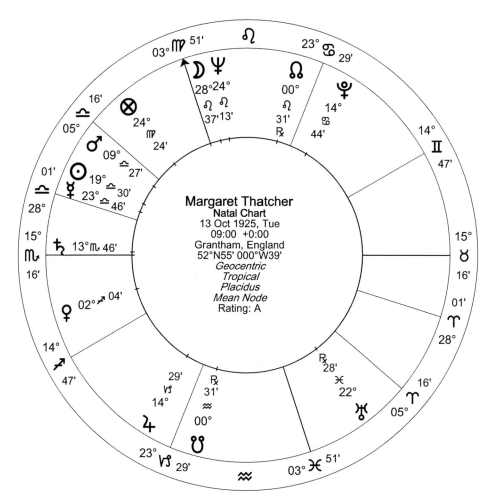

If Margaret Thatcher had come to you as a client how could you have advised her? You could have suggested that she increase the size of her capital 'I' which would have allowed her to examine her Saturn conjunct the Ascendant and the ramifications of her sense of inferiority. You could have encouraged her to lower the size of the 't' and draw the cross bar firmly attached to the top, crossing it left to right and inclined slightly upwards. This would have lowered her sights to goals more easily achieved and thus given her a greater sense of satisfaction in her work. You could also have suggested she form her 'f's in a more conventional fashion, rather than as a figure 8 or propeller 'f'. This would have relaxed the pressure she placed on herself and helped her to be happier with her success, giving her more opportunities to explore the charisma, intuition, and inspiration of her Moon-Neptune conjunction square to Venus. The ramifications for her as leader would have been immense.

6

The Handwriting in the Chart

In the previous chapter we considered the handwriting and looked for its correlation in the natal chart. We can also do the reverse. By considering the broad brush stroke issues in a chart we can anticipate what we might see in the handwriting. Any mismatch will then tell us what behavioural issues require work.

Meet Andrew ...

Andrew came for a consultation in mid-1995. Two weeks previously he had lost his job as manager of a company specializing in graphic arts and web design and was still in shock.

The separate issues of Andrew's chart are as follows:

1. Meticulous approach to the world. With a Virgo Ascendant he is seen by others as someone who is careful, analytical and fastidious. He may also be seen as somebody who is unduly preoccupied with personal health, believing that illness is nearly always present or imminent. Born in 1952, Andrew is part of the Saturn-Neptune generation which fears the loss of established structures in society, the consequences of which, at worst, can result in corruptions such as malpractice or misdiagnosis in western medicine. With Saturn conjunct Neptune in the first house forming part of a T-Square, this is another indicator of weakened health in a chart.

⬥ **What might I expect to see in his handwriting?** His handwriting may be extremely neat, sitting mostly in the practical plains landscape, it may be tight and rigid, reflecting his fear of making mistakes, it may be full of angles, showing his critical, analytical side, or it may display an earthy sensuality with rounded letters (Virgo Ascendant). He might also use a light pressure in his handwriting, demonstrating reduced vitality (Saturn-Neptune).

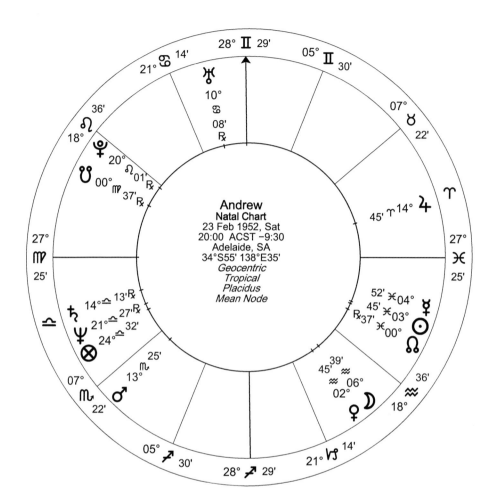

2. **The ability to proactively solve his own career problems** (angular cardinal T-Square: Saturn-Neptune conjunction in the 1st house in opposition to Jupiter in the 7th house and both square to Uranus in the 10th house). This aspect is proactive (Neptune trine MC) and challenge-oriented (cardinal), demanding responsibility (exalted Saturn rising in the chart) and risk-taking (Jupiter-Uranus) in personal relationships as well as business and career. It also contains possible health difficulties when under stress (Saturn-Neptune). In its best-case scenario this T-square can be shaped into a graphic arts business which embraces his spiritual or artistic vision.

◈ **What might I expect to see in his handwriting?** His handwriting might show a right slant and an openness on the page, with wide margins and good spacing between the words and lines.

3. Creative talent. As he engages with the T-Square, he gains the gift of the water Grand Trine (Sun-Mercury-North Node in the 6th house trine Uranus in the 10th house trine Mars in the 2nd house). This carries an immense creative talent (Sun-Mercury in Pisces) which draws on his insightful and unusual ideas (Mercury-Uranus) and it is these ideas and concepts that energize the chart (Mars-Uranus) and give him his sense of independence (Sun-Uranus) and fulfilment (North Node).

◈   **What might I expect to see in his handwriting?** His handwriting might show rounded letters in the practical plains region, as well as a fount of emotion through large loops pushing down into the valleys.

4. Motivation and drive from hidden family issues (Fixed square: Mars in the 2nd house square Pluto in the 12th house). One of Andrew's greatest resources (Mars in rulership in the 2nd house ruling the 2nd house) is an immense vigour which strengthens and irrevocably changes him (Mars-Pluto). This aspect requires him to be physically active in order to avoid health problems from blocked anger or rage. The difficulty is that he comes from a family that avoids confronting the deeper matters of life (Pluto in the 12th house), possibly as a result of an abuse of power by one of his ancestors (Jupiter trine Pluto and Pluto in the 12th house). Thus he may, in a reversal of this aspect, experience blocked anger or rage that erupts unexpectedly from people against him. The South Node, although in a different sign, is also in the 12th house, reiterating family issues which may be hidden from him.

◈   **What might I expect to see in his handwriting?** His handwriting might show hooks on the ends of letters, letters that would normally begin in the practical landscape beginning instead in the valleys, angles on letters that sweep into the valleys, or left luggage in his script.

5. Motivation and drive through emotional independence and social networking (Fixed succeedent square: Mars in Scorpio in the 2nd house square the Moon in Aquarius in the 5th house. The Moon is also conjunct Venus in Aquarius). This succeedent square means he makes money (Mars in Scorpio in the 2nd house) steadily and practically (fixed) from being personally creative and emotionally independent (Mars-Moon in Aquarius). He also gains emotional satisfaction from graphic design or creative social networks (Venus in Aquarius in the 5th house conjunct the Moon).

◈   **What might I expect to see in his handwriting?** His handwriting might show a bow-and-arrow 'f', a creative 'g' or it may contain angular writing in the plains landscape, showing his love of ideas and concepts.

Here is Andrew's handwriting:

Andrew's writing is balanced on the page with spacious margins and ample space between the words and the lines, so he listens to others and he allows new ideas into his thinking, suggesting either the intuitive reception of Mercury in Pisces as part of the water Grand Trine, or else the emotional satisfaction he gains from new ideas and concepts (Moon in Aquarius square Mars). The slant and drive of the handwriting is to the right, showing general enthusiasm and optimism (Jupiter-Uranus willingness to take risks) and the letters are composed as 'friendly writing' with soft undulations: Andrew reaches out to people (the gregariousness suggested by his Venus in Aquarius square Mars in Scorpio).

In contrast, his writing on the left begins large and then flattens out as he moves to the right, seen particularly clearly in the words 'appointment' and 'Regards', implying that he starts with enthusiasm but may be intimidated by the future (Pluto in the 12th house as fear of change).

His 't' bars sit mostly in his mountain landscape, so he sets his goals at what he feels is a manageable height for him, and they are written to the right of the stem, so he finishes projects well (cardinal T-Square with its exalted Saturn).

However, there are no dreams or goals when he writes the letter 'f'. The emphasized lower loop in his valley landscape is indicative of someone who helps others to achieve their dreams and feels he has no capacity to manifest his own. He also writes the loop of the letter 'f' with a backwards motion, suggesting an unconscious desire to sabotage his plans. All the good work he achieves with his exalted Saturn is eroded by Neptune. Given this, it is appropriate to see if any of his letters carry a resentment stroke. The capital 'A' of his signature begins with a fishing line into his emotions, which signifies that he holds onto past emotional experiences and that it damages his goals and aspirations, as that is where it is released. Reinforcing this is the lake of held emotions created by the loop forming the cross stroke within the capital 'A'; and whilst the long final stroke of the 'w' shows initiative and enterprise, enthusiasm and a willingness to try new ideas, it ends in a small knot indicating an unconscious blockade.

The long, over-emphasized loops in the valleys of the letters 'y', 'g' and capital 'J' of 'July' indicates someone dominated by their instincts and reveals the strength of the water Grand Trine and the Sun-Mercury-North Node in Pisces in the 6th house.

There is left luggage in the letters 'o' (totally encircled), 'p', capital 'D' on 'Deposit' and in capital 'S' and 'a' of 'Saturday', so there are hidden issues and family voices that strangle him (Pluto in the 12th house) as well as rules and regulations (South Node in Virgo in the 12th house) that bind him to the past.

The exaggerated capital letters 'D', 'F', 'J' point towards Andrew trying to make an impression or compensating for an inferiority complex in order to reinforce his self-esteem (Pluto in the 12th and the ruler of his 2nd house).

Overall the handwriting shows someone who has all the will in the world to achieve their own goals but has been forced by life to achieve other people's goals instead, with attached feelings of intimidation and resentment.

What can Andrew do?

Andrew came to see me in July 1995, a year after his secondary progressed Moon had entered his 12th house and from which it was not due to emerge for another eighteen months. He was also in the Gibbous phase of adjustment prior to the phase becoming Full in 1997. The incoming Pluto transit squaring his nodal axis, transiting through his 2nd house (Pluto natally in the 12th and having an affinity with his 2nd house), highlighted profound changes to his personal resources. Ahead of him in 1996 lay transiting Uranus conjunct his Venus, occurring in his 5th house, with Uranus natally in the 10th house and having an affinity with the 6th house. This augured well for changes to his financial situation through his career. Faced with the potently real challenge of finding work that would bring him an income, now was the time for Andrew to readjust the sails of his vessel (Gibbous phase) and decide what it was he wanted to achieve with the rest of his life.

There were several areas of his handwriting that he could change to help the transits manifest to his advantage. He could begin by making a list of his short term and long term goals and then start reaching for them by adding mountain sweeps to his letters 'f' and 'l', at the same time changing his reversed 'f' to one that moved forward in direction. He could make his letters a consistent size across the page so that he was actively embracing the future, rather than feeling browbeaten by it. He could slowly diminish the size of his capitals. Finally he could raise the bar on his 't' right to the top and begin drawing it evenly from left to right.

As he made those changes to his handwriting, so Andrew needed to realise that he would be unleashing issues which may have remained dormant for years, particularly issues to do with Pluto in his 12th house. Nevertheless the transits suggested intense change and chaos and this was a good way to use them.

Andrew's predictive astrology

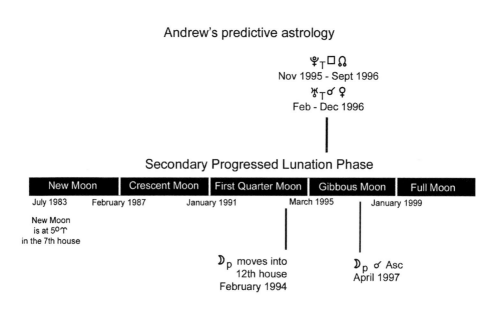

Meet Judy …

Judy wrote to Astro Logos in late 1999 requesting a copy of her birth chart. Whilst she was not a client, her handwriting presented an interesting pattern, and so I kept it amongst my examples. She has given me permission to use it as a teaching tool.

The separate issues of Judy's chart are as follows:

1. A yielding approach to the world powered by the drive for education (Pisces Ascendant with Jupiter, its ruler, square to Mars and Mars square Pluto). With a Pisces Ascendant, Judy is seen by others as someone who is empathic and sensitive, compliant to the needs of those around her, and having a chameleon-like persona. It also implies the need for emotional security running through

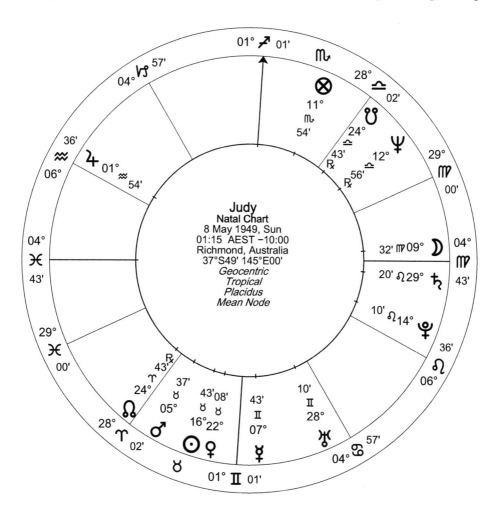

her life as a background theme. Yet driving this need is a determined (fixed square) and practical realization of ideas (Mars in Taurus in the 3rd house) gained through education (Mars ruling the 3rd and Scorpio intercepted in the 9th house) as well as from groups, either learning from them or teaching them (Jupiter in Aquarius in the 11th house). This part of Judy also connects to a vibrant strength (Mars-Pluto) which has to be shaped and fashioned into physical expression. This can help her ideas take physical form, particularly if used for and on behalf of others (cadent square). If, however, this energy is blocked in any way, it can lead to health problems, such as excessive cell growth or a crisis with her immune system, a predicament which can be greatly helped by slow, measured (fixed square) physical activities such as yoga or T'ai Chi (Mars in Taurus square Pluto).

◈ **What might I expect to see in her handwriting?** Her handwriting might show a light pressure (indicating the pliant nature of the Ascendant), or it might show heavy pressure (indicating the strength of the Mars-Pluto). It might show letters, words and lines that are separated, allowing the thoughts and ideas of others to flow amongst her own (Mars in the 3rd house square Jupiter in Aquarius in the 11th house), or her handwriting might be written as block capitals (showing the obstructing influence of the Mars in Taurus square Pluto).

2. **The road to self-empowerment** (Sun-Venus conjunction in Taurus in the 3rd house square Pluto in the 6th house). This part of Judy describes her ego, identity and vitality. It has been modelled by a father figure whom she experiences as a paradox: teaching her reliance on the material comforts of the non-changing world (Sun-Venus in Taurus) whilst dealing with upheaval and issues of trust and betrayal (Sun-Pluto/Venus-Pluto). As the planets are in a cadent square, Judy is able to realize this part of her chart by working for and on behalf of others who are also dealing with such dilemmas.

◈ **What might I expect to see in her handwriting?** Her handwriting might be written in block capitals, showing stubbornness and resistance to change (Sun-Venus in Taurus with Venus in rulership), or be positioned mainly in the practical plains region. It may show an earthy sensuality through a calligraphic pen, or one that has a large footprint (Sun-Venus in Taurus with Venus in rulership). Her handwriting may be slanted to the left, indicating a history of hurt or of having been let down and wanting to hold onto the past, or contain hooks in the valley landscape of her emotions, or areas of left luggage of buried hurt (Sun-Pluto/Venus-Pluto). It may also contain 't' bars crossed to the right of the stem indicating her ability to work for and on behalf of others and that she is able to complete projects (cadency).

3. **Learning from her partner how to shape her imaginative ideas** (Moon in Virgo in 7th house square Mercury in Gemini in the 4th house, Mercury making a Grand Trine with Jupiter and Neptune). The tension produced between home and partner, thinking and feeling, forces her to take action (square) to find a way of articulating her talent (trine) for imaginative and creative thinking (Mercury trine Neptune). This may be obstructed by the voices of early maternal criticism or judgement (Moon in Virgo in 7th square Mercury), initially experienced as the emotional worries of her mother (Moon is in the 7th house in Virgo) and then of every partner with whom she forms an intimate relationship. Therefore this part of Judy has to learn to think clearly whilst feeling, and in so doing, find clear boundaries which can contain her big ideas (Mercury trine Jupiter).

❖ **What might I expect to see in her handwriting?** Her handwriting might show openness to ideas reflected in openly spaced letters (Mercury-Jupiter), or creative letters such as figure of eight 'g' or a clear 'd' (Mercury-Neptune). It may also contain angles, indicative of critical or analytical thinking (Moon in Virgo square Mercury in Gemini).

4. **Opportunities to structure her unconventional ideas** (Saturn in Leo in the 6th house sextile Uranus in 4th house). This part of Judy brings her opportunities to break new ground with the help of others (Saturn in detriment). However, being an unaspected duet, these opportunities may be erratic and she may find that sometimes she has a great deal of determination and persistence and at other times none at all.

❖ **What might I expect to see in her handwriting?** Her handwriting might show her determination in the way she crosses her 't', forcefully and fully across the top from left to right. It may show her reaching for her goals and dreams by letters stretching up into the mountain landscape. It may also show a lack of structure (the 'on again-off again' nature of an unaspected planet or duet) through a light pressure or a low 't' cross-bar.

5. **Finding her independent resources.** Through the journey of her nodal axis, Judy will seek her own independent personal resources in her early twenties (North Node in Aries in the 2nd house). Part of those resources will be learning how to effectively shape her ideas through education (Mars in the 3rd house as dispositor of the North Node square Pluto and Jupiter). However, in her late twenties-early thirties she comes to understand that she does not have the depth of maturity to maintain this position of self-determination and has to learn how to work with others and become skilled in the processes of consensus (South

Node in Libra in the 8th house). In so doing she has to face issues of trust and betrayal in friendships and intimate relationships (dispositor of the South Node is Venus conjunct the Sun in Taurus and square Pluto). In this manner she gains strength in following and trusting her own practical pathway, and so she gains the independence she sought in her early twenties.

◈   **What might I expect to see in her handwriting?** Her handwriting might show a lean towards the right, indicating the love of challenge (North Node in Aries) or the heavy pressure of assertion (Mars-Pluto); or it may contain the open spaces of receptivity and harmony and a light pressure showing balance and harmony (South Node in Libra); or it may be slanted to the left, or contain hooks in the valley landscape of her emotions (Sun-Pluto/Venus-Pluto).

Here is Judy's handwriting:

Yes please - thanks so much.

my birth was at 1·15 am

at richmond (near melbourne)

on   8|5|1949

stunning post card

hooray

judy

cheeky me ° -

my kids were born

on 19/3/1971 in

melbourne at 6·20 pm

and on 1/1/1981 in

melbourne at 3·20pm,

my important man

was born on 8/8/1947

in melbourne at in

mid afternoon.

be well, happy &

peaceful, heh?

The predominant feature of Judy's handwriting is its openness on the page, indicating that she listens to people and welcomes new ideas (air trine between Jupiter in Aquarius in the 11th house and Mercury in Gemini in the 4th house). However, apart from the initial capital 'y' of 'Yes', she uses lower case letters throughout. This disconnected writing in its best expression suggests thinking that is influenced by intuition or feeling (Moon-Mercury), as well as self-reliance and independence (North Node in Aries). In its more difficult expression it can indicate scattered thinking and lack of concentration (air trine between Mercury and Jupiter), along with a desire for seclusion and/or wariness of others (Sun-

Venus square Pluto). This desire to withdraw and its associated loneliness is reiterated in the slope of her letters which lean slightly to the left.

Horizontally her handwriting contains an undulating wave pattern which starts and ends at about the same height, showing a capacity to make use of opportunities and reach her goals (Saturn sextile Uranus). However, since the cross bars of her letter 't' sit to the right of the stem in the practical landscape, these goals are not necessarily hers to achieve. Indeed whilst the cross bars slope upwards, showing optimism, the way Judy writes her 't' suggests that she prefers to complete projects that others begin (cadency). Judy sets goals high enough for her to manage but nothing beyond what she can comfortably reach.

This is emphasized by the fact that the bulk of her letters sit in the plains landscape. There are no loops sweeping into the mountains, implying that her dreams and aspirations are muted, and no lower loops cascading into her valleys, suggesting that her emotions are carefully corralled. In fact the mountain loops on her 'f' denote dreams and goals without practical application (Pisces Ascendant/Mercury-Neptune), even though in Judy's chart there is the ability for the practical realization of ideas (Mars in Taurus in the 3rd house) through education (Mars ruling the 3rd and Scorpio intercepted in the 9th house) and groups (Jupiter in Aquarius in the 11th house).

Instead the letter that does form a loop as it plunges into the valleys of her emotions is the letter 'p' ('please', 'postcard', 'pm' and 'important'). Since such a letter does not usually carry a loop, this is one place where Judy consciously or unconsciously buries emotions from the past, since it is formed to the left of the letter in both the emotional and practical landscapes (Sun-Venus square Pluto). There is also left luggage in Judy's colons and 'i' dots which are written as circles. Opinion is divided on the meaning of this, since it is often found in the handwriting of adolescent girls, suggesting immaturity and the desire for attention, hence unrecognized and unconscious emotional issues. However, it is also found in the handwriting of artists, designers and architects as a way of expressing uniqueness.

On sample 1 the left margin moves steadily to the right, indicating spontaneity and enthusiasm or else impatience. The lack of right margins on both pieces of handwriting suggest she rushes towards her future with a desire for involvement and communication (Moon in the 7th house in Virgo/Moon square Mercury/air trine between Mercury and Jupiter) and the addition of 'my' in 'my birth' inserted later reiterates her pattern of rapid thinking, wanting to get words down quickly.

Overall there is a child-like quality to the writing, emphasized by the smiling face with a heart in the centre (Pisces Ascendant), on the one hand an innocent delight in life, on the other an unconscious written request not to be hurt (Sun-Venus square Pluto).

This is Judy's handwriting now:

I'm a lapsed secondary teacher
a passionate biodynamic farmer
was dumped 4 a goldilocks
mother of 2 wondrous souls – kate
delivered bondy when she was 10.
backpacked greece & turkey with bondy when he was 10
slept on kate's floor on santorini island
am an indigo child
so is bondy
built a mud brick house after making the
bricks
now building strawbale – earth floor
a lapsed agnostic
died a couple of times when a drunk driver
collected us – brought back 2 life – hooray
recently finished a masters
happily putting together a doctorate on
agricultural biodynamics combined with the joy of
most WWOOFers (willing workers on organic farms)
am besotted by the desert
" " " arty-farty films (eat them up)
love 2 write 4 publications
wrote 4 the local rag (pony club news) 4 about
5 yrs before the smash interrupted that.
love walking, travelling, jogging, interacting,
chatting, investigating nature, dogs, chooks, horses, cows,
compost, weeds, fruit, veggies, special folk, everything

delivered bondy when she was 10.
backpacked greece & turkey with bondy when he was 10
slept on kate's floor on santorini island
am an indigo child

The most noticeable difference in Judy's handwriting in 2008 is that her letters 'g' and 'y' now contain sweeps down into her valley landscape, suggesting that her emotional nature – her deep feelings, sentiments and passions – is now finding better articulation in her life. Her lines of handwriting now slant upwards indicating an optimistic attitude to life. Her letter 'p' contains far less luggage. Finally the writing has a much wider left hand margin, suggesting more of a willingness to engage with life. The overall impression is that Judy's life has become more enriched emotionally. This may be attributed to the fact that she has gained her Masters degree and is now working towards her doctorate.

Judy's path ahead

In 2009 Judy's secondary Progressed Moon moves into its Gibbous phase (a time of adjustment), into Sagittarius (a broader view of the world) and across her MC (changes in how society sees and judges her place in the world). Being the year of her fifth Jupiter Return, it emphasizes growth through learning, teaching and education. This, then, is a year of optimism and joy (transiting Jupiter squares her natal Venus) which reshapes her place in the world (progressed Moon-MC).

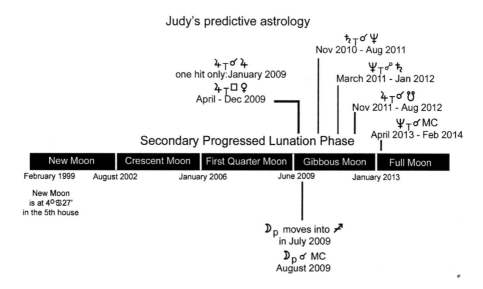

Judy's predictive astrology

Looking ahead, from November 2010 – February 2012 there are health issues which require her attention (transiting Saturn conjunct Neptune, transiting Neptune opposition Saturn and transiting Jupiter conjunct the South Node) and in 2013 her status in the world is again reshaped, this time either by loss, confusion and despair or through the arts, healing, and metaphysics (transiting Neptune conjunct the MC).

With four planets and a luminary in cadent houses, and a luminary in the 7th house, the astrology suggests that Judy prefers to work with others and help them to achieve their dreams as her way of gaining satisfaction in the world. However, Judy has her natal Mercury in rulership and angular, so this period of working on her doctorate is a time when she could, if she so wished, make the following changes in her handwriting:

She could change her half letter 'f' to a full 'f' to ground her ideas more fully and allow the work of her doctorate to come to fruition. She could also extend the bar of her letter 't' across the whole letter and begin to raise it up to the top of the stem and angle it up slightly. As she brought in these changes to her handwriting, so she literally and continually sees in front of her on the page the goals towards which she strives. This then becomes a mirror for her internal changes, helping to steer the course of her doctorate towards greater success as her secondary Progressed Moon sweeps over her MC. In sum, these changes could help to reveal her 'netivot' more clearly, enabling her doctoral work to be seen.

Meet 'Lydia' ...

When Lydia was twenty years old she won a national charity contest. The title gave her the opportunity to travel and represent Australia as an ambassador overseas. However, being in the public eye was not a pleasant experience for her and when she returned home at the end of her year of travel, she married Harry and settled down to wedded life, preferring to forget the whole episode. In 1994 Lydia began studying astrology with Astro Logos.

The separate issues of Lydia's chart are as follows:

1. A practical, sensual approach to the world informed by intensity. With a Taurus Ascendant Lydia is seen by others as someone who is realistic, reliable and steadfast, as well as someone who is open to the sensory rhythms of her environment. She could also be seen as somebody who is fearful of allowing change into her world. This may be explained by a difficult and dramatic beginning to life (ruler of the Ascendant, Venus in Capricorn, conjunct the Moon in Capricorn and both trine Pluto), the consequence of being born to an older mother or one who has little energy (Moon in Capricorn), resulting in a bond with mother that is, on the one hand, deeply emotional and non-superficial, and on the other, emotionally distant (Moon trine Uranus). Thus Lydia experiences her mother as someone who struggles with the concept of emotional intimacy (Moon in Capricorn/Moon trine Uranus) and so Lydia feels both unable to get close to her mother (Moon in Capricorn) and yet overwhelmed by her emotionally (Moon

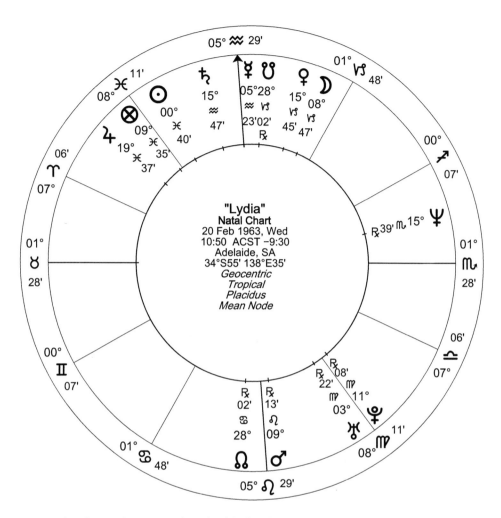

"Lydia"
Natal Chart
20 Feb 1963, Wed
10:50 ACST −9:30
Adelaide, SA
34°S55' 138°E35'
Geocentric
Tropical
Placidus
Mean Node

trine Pluto). Furthermore this double-bind is connected to a fear of relating or shyness (Moon conjunct Venus in Capricorn). When Lydia is older, she can turn this fear into a skill at socializing and networking, balancing emotional intensity and loyalty (Moon-Pluto/Venus-Pluto) with emotional independence (Moon-Uranus) and empathy (partile Venus sextile Neptune).

◈   **What might I expect to see in her handwriting?** Her handwriting might show fear of letting go of the material world through cramped letters or 't' bars placed low on the stem. It may show separation anxiety (Moon in Capricorn) through handwriting that hugs the left hand margin. It may also offer undulations that form a chalice (Venus-Moon/Venus-Neptune) indicating someone who collects ideas, stories, people, and objects.

2. Learning from her partner how to maintain clear boundaries (angular fixed T-Square: Mars-Saturn/Mars-Mercury with Neptune as the apex planet in the 7th house). This problem-solving tool in Lydia's chart gives her the ability to take on a great deal of hard work (Mars-Saturn) from an early age (Saturn in the 10th house) in an effort to give form and shape to her ideas (Mars-Mercury). However, she learns from her parents' relationship that such energy can easily be undermined by her partner (Neptune in the 7th house square Mars). This is an unconscious family pattern with which Lydia struggles her whole life (Mars in the 4th conjunct the IC is the ruler of both the 12th house and the 7th house). She also wrestles with taking on the responsibility of a career versus serving her husband's career (Saturn in the 10th ruling the 10th) and such a struggle may undermine her health (Saturn square Neptune) or force her to look after his health. As a result Lydia may express this as marrying or forming a business partnership with someone who is, in worst case scenario, irresponsible as well as ill, or a dreamer, or an alcoholic, or else, in best case scenario, is someone who is highly responsible and is also religious or spiritual or works in the metaphysical or healing fields.

◈ **What might I expect to see in her handwriting?** Her handwriting might show an excess of letters that travel into the emotional, primal valleys of her landscape (Neptune as apex of T-Square). It may show a self-sabotage 'f' or oversize capitals in an attempt to shore up feelings of inadequacy (Saturn in rulership in the 10th house ruling the 10th in opposition to Mars). It may show areas of left luggage where family patterns are still unconsciously causing obstruction (Mars in the 4th ruling the 12th in opposition to Saturn). It may display angularity in the plains landscape, allowing her intellect prominence (Mercury in Aquarius conjunct the MC in opposition to Mars).

3. The challenge of independence and intellect balanced with empathy (Sun in Pisces in the 10th house opposition Uranus in the 4th house). This part of Lydia describes her ego, identity and vitality and has been modelled on a father-figure whom she sees either as eccentric (Sun-Uranus) and disempowered (Sun in Pisces), or else highly empathic and creative (Sun in Pisces) and independent (Sun-Uranus).

◈ **What might I expect to see in her handwriting?** Her handwriting might show her unique creativity through a figure of eight 'g', or her fluid ideas through a ligature 'th'. It may also encapsulate letters that dive deeply into the valleys of her life (Sun in Pisces ruling the IC). Counterbalancing this, her writing may display her intellect through angularity (Sun-Uranus).

4. The thirst for education. Through the journey of her nodal axis Lydia will look for a way of caring for or cherishing people in her local neighbourhood (North Node in Cancer in the 3rd house) and will achieve success in this field in her early twenties. In accessing this part of her chart, however, she will encounter the emotions connected with her own difficult birth scenario (Moon as dispositor of the North Node conjunct Venus and trine Uranus-Pluto) and in her late twenties-early thirties come to understand that what she lacks is the broader knowledge base necessary for sustaining her position (South Node in Capricorn in the 9th house) and may utilize travel, publishing or higher learning to achieve this. In so doing she will have to face issues of responsibility and of her own authority (Saturn as dispositor of the South Node in rulership in the 10th house ruling the 9th and 10th houses).

◈ **What might I expect to see in her handwriting?** Her handwriting might show the undulations of friendly writing that wants to reach out to others and nurture them (Cancer North Node) or it may show 't' bars placed at the top of the letter as she takes on the responsibility of learning and knowledge (Capricorn South Node).

Here is Lydia's handwriting in 1996:

Dear Darelyn —
Please find enclosed a cheque for $70 as
payment for 'the 1996 Winter School in Delineation'.
Many, many thanks for a fabulous Unit 3!
See you soon —
"The Karate Kid"! ☺

Lydia's margins all around are balanced, indicating that she has a good sense of space and of how she locates herself in the world. There is an upward slant to the lines signifying optimism and a forward slant to the letters representative of enthusiasm. She writes her 'th' ('thanks') with a ligature, demonstrating fluid thinking.

However, her handwriting displays oversized lower loops ballooning deeply into the valleys of her world on her 'y' and 'f' letters, suggesting that there are emotional issues with which she is still struggling, or of which she is unaware. Long loops like this can also indicate someone who feels ineffective and so seeks privacy and seclusion. As well, the bases of some letters whose shapes would normally stay within the practical area of the plains fall into these valleys, such as swollen loops on capital 'D', capital S ('See you') and capital T ('The').

Sweeps into the mountains of the top of the letter 'f' are almost non-existent. They also carry excess luggage with the extra loop in the central plains. This excess luggage also occurs on the top of the letter 'o' and at the bottom of the letter 's' and the centre of her capital 'K'. Finally the bars of her crossed letter 't' are all located in her plains landscape.

What can Lydia do?

How can she help improve these devitalising parts of her chart? In examining her predictive work there are a number of matters to consider. In the middle of 1996 Lydia was just beginning a Secondary Progressed New Moon Lunation Phase, so this was an excellent time to implement changes in her handwriting as a way of signalling her readiness to alter her circumstances and plant the seeds of her new direction in life. It occurred at 4 degrees Aries in the 11th house, her Secondary Progressed Sun having moved into Aries in 1992, so this pathway was one of independence and assertion connected with groups of people.

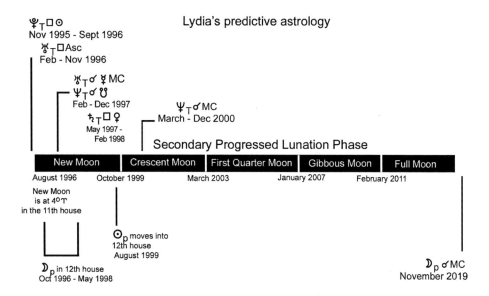

Her transits in 1996 were also about change: a drive for freedom (transiting Uranus square her Ascendant), and irrevocable changes to her identity and vitality (transiting Pluto square her Sun). In 1997 she would experience changes to her thinking and her place in the world (transiting Uranus conjunct her Mercury and MC) and revisit an issue or person from her past with spiritual, metaphysical or creative connections (transiting Neptune conjunct her South Node). This also coincided with changes to her commitments (transiting Saturn square to Venus).

In October 1996 Lydia's Secondary Progressed Moon went into the 12th house and stayed there until May 1998, offering her plenty of time out of the public eye to make these adjustments, followed by her Secondary Progressed Sun moving into her 12th house in 1999, allowing her to make an even greater connection with her inner life. Looking further ahead to 2000, she then gains the opportunity to establish a career in the arts, healing or metaphysics (transiting Neptune conjunct her MC).

Other landmarks to note were her Secondary Progressed Lunation Phase becoming Full in 2011 and her Secondary Progressed Moon moving over her MC in 2019. Whatever Lydia was seeding in 1996 would gain her initial success in 2011 and slowly increase towards a more substantial success in 2019. Whilst this seemed a long way off, future plans can only come to fruition through planning a path towards them and readjusting as they emerge.

By consciously focusing on restructuring her letter 'f' to make two equally balanced mountain and valley loops and eliminating the hooks and containers in the plains landscape, Lydia can begin to consider her own dreams and goals and to set about making them happen, rather than maintaining service to her family or her husband. At the same time she could diminish the size of the loops sweeping into her valleys in the letter 'y' and in letters which do not usually contain loops such as in capital 'D' and capital 'S'. In this way she starts to bring her unconscious family pattern regarding drive and ambition and the expression of new ideas (Mars, the ruler of the 12th house in the 4th house opposing Saturn and Mercury) into a more conscious framework. She could also raise the bar on every letter 't' and set her sights high to accomplish the promise of her 10th house Saturn in rulership as part of the T-Square.

What happened to Lydia?
In 2000, as transiting Neptune crossed her MC, Lydia began a Ph.D. in Creative Writing, taking the opportunity to explore through writing her experience of early fame. She completed that in 2005, corresponding with the years covering her mid-life crisis transits of transiting Pluto square Pluto (2000), transiting Uranus opposition Uranus (2004) and transiting Neptune square Neptune (2005). In 2008 Lydia wrote to me:

> I am proud of my Ph.D. I found the process totally rewarding, mind-altering, stimulating, challenging and was well-supported within the university for my work. My extraordinary supervisor became my dearest friend. My novel about the pitfalls of fame and fortune has not been published yet. I've only approached Australian publishers to date and feel I need to go overseas with it.
>
> Harry and I continue to have a fulfilling marriage. We now have two large businesses in South Australia (both in the field of alternative health practices) and I am enjoying my role as co-director with Harry. I am also exploring art now at art school and I'm absolutely loving it. My work in 2007 received High Distinctions from notoriously rigorous teachers so that has encouraged me a lot! I'm looking to do my first art exhibition (painting) in 2008. I'd also like to paint the themes of my book and compose music for an exhibition in 2009. I am still fundraising for the Moon Bears with a stunning group of women but haven't been to China yet. That's an adventure still to come. In the meantime I am adopting Beagles in need of rehoming (long story!).

This is Lydia's handwriting in 2007-8:
Having achieved her goal of her doctorate and now pursuing her art with an eye to exhibiting and publishing, Lydia's handwriting in 2007-08 displays many constructive changes. Her letter 'f' is now much more balanced in all three of her landscapes and she has almost completely eliminated the ballooning loops sweeping into her valleys. Indeed the only full valley loop occurs in the word 'you' of 'reconnect with you', revealing an emotional connection with the receiver of

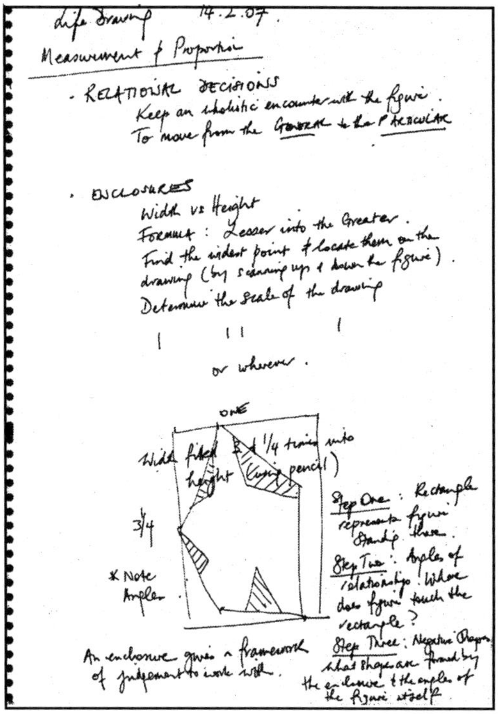

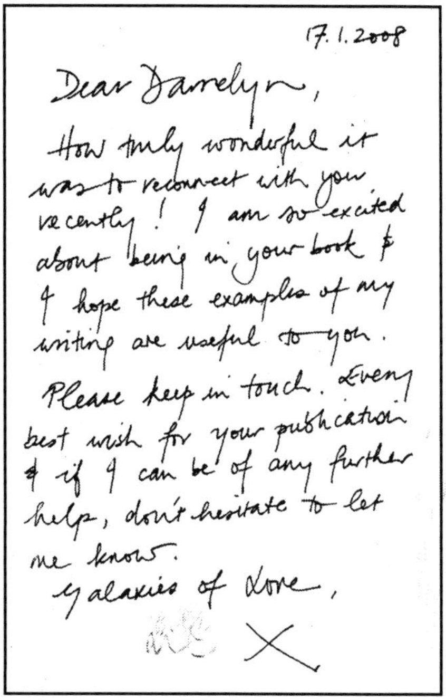

17. 1. 2008

Dear Jarrelyn,

How truly wonderful it
was to reconnect with you
recently! I am so excited

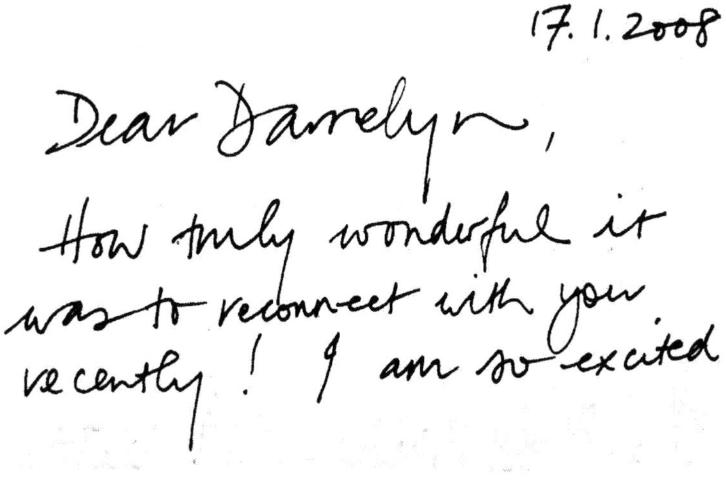

the letter, thus acting as a positive trigger word in bringing to light a joyful past history. Overall Lydia's handwriting expresses a great deal more confidence than it did in 1996: the margins on the right and left hand sides are more balanced; there is equal spacing between the individual words and between the lines of handwriting, indicating clarity of thought, organizing ability, and a balanced perspective; her capital letter 'I' is written with a straight finishing stroke demonstrating her sense of independence; and her letters 'h' and 'l' include more substantial sweeps into her mountain landscape, suggesting that her personal goals have become much clearer and more significant to her.

Amongst her other goals, Lydia's ambition is to exhibit her painting, paint the themes of her book and compose music for her work. In 2011 transiting Neptune conjuncts Lydia's Sun (reshaping her identity through art, music and writing) as the Secondary Progressed Lunation phase becomes Full (working hard to harvest what has been produced). Along with the changes she has already made to her handwriting, Lydia can begin to raise the cross-bar of her letter 't' so that she achieves the best success that she can in this active, assertive phase of her life. As Lydia continues to adjust her handwriting and make changes, so she takes action in concert with her predictive work to co-create her pathway, and so her 'netivot' are slowly revealed to her.

Meet 'Angela'...

Angela came to me as a client in late 2006. She was already established in her field as a Life Coach but her recent move from her home town was bringing up issues of sadness embedded in her past. Her loss history included the death of her paternal grandmother at age five, the death of her father at age sixteen, the death of her paternal grandfather at age thirty, and the death of her youngest son from cancer at the age of six when she was forty. She now wanted a better understanding of the motifs of loss and grief in her chart.

The separate issues of Angela's chart are as follows:

1. **Passionate communication as an approach to the world.** As with Andrew, who also has a Virgo Ascendant, Angela is seen by others as someone who is careful, analytical and fastidious. She may also be seen as somebody who is unduly preoccupied with personal health and believes that illness is nearly always present or imminent. As with Andrew, a background theme running through her life is the need for material security (earth Ascendant) and one of the ways she will achieve this is through her thinking, writing and communication skills (the ruler of her Ascendant is Mercury). However, unlike Andrew, people recognize within Angela the ability to inspire them using her highly-focused and penetrating mind in a process-oriented environment such as counselling or analysis (Mercury in Leo conjunct Pluto conjunct the Ascendant). The difficulty she faces with this part of her chart is that she has never been taught appropriate ways of handling loss, for this is a death-denying family (Pluto in the 12th house). So the tools she will be drawn to developing in herself will be those of counselling and processing, for these allow her to consider loss from many different perspectives.

❖ **What might I expect to see in her handwriting?** Her handwriting may be large and contain finials and/or embellishments, expressing flamboyance (Mercury in Leo). It may also contain the heavy pressure of persistence and focus (Mercury-Pluto).

2. **Security needs**. Another way that she seeks to make herself physically secure (earth Ascendant) is through the acquisition of material goods which may have been denied her as a child (unaspected Saturn in the 2nd house). The capacity to work hard in a creative way (Capricorn is intercepted in the 5th house and Saturn rules the 6th house) is a resource that Angela values but due to its on-again /off-again quality, she may have difficulty relying on it until she learns how to turn the 'switch' on at will. So another loss motif in her chart may be survivor guilt and feelings of inadequacy at not being able to hold on to her resources.

❖ **What might I expect to see in her handwriting?** She may write in block letters, emphasizing a restriction of resources (Saturn in the 2nd house). She may cross her letter 't' in the plains landscape, reaching only as high as she believes she deserves to achieve.

3. **The ability to pro-actively solve group issues** (T-Square: Jupiter in the 8th house, close to the 9th house cusp and in the same sign as it, is in opposition to Neptune in the 3rd house, and both are square to Mars conjunct Uranus in Cancer in the 11th house). Through taking on the challenge (cardinal) and change of education (3rd-9th axis and Jupiter natally in the 8th house) and teaching (Jupiter-Neptune), Angela has the ability to motivate large groups of people (Mars conjunct Uranus in the 11th house). This will have repercussions for the way she handles her own anger and emotions (Mars-Uranus/Mars in Cancer), ricocheting into issues connected with her libido (Mars-Neptune), and driving her to develop clear boundaries between herself and others. In this way she learns how to stay invigorated when with other people, rather than feeling drained by them (Mars-Neptune), which will allow her to reach for her goals by taking risks (Jupiter-Uranus).

❖ **What might I expect to see in her handwriting?** Her handwriting may show the letter 't' crossed at the top (the challenges of the cardinal T-Square and the risk-taking of the Jupiter-Uranus). Her letters in general may be open rather than compressed, particularly the letters 'h', 'm', and 'n' (the Mars-Uranus group interaction). On the other hand, feeling drained of energy, her lines of handwriting may slant downwards or be light in pressure (Mars-Neptune).

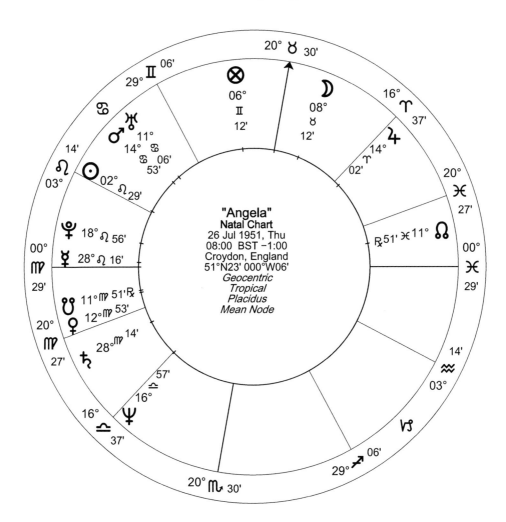

"Angela"
Natal Chart
26 Jul 1951, Thu
08:00 BST −1:00
Croydon, England
51°N23' 000°W06'
Geocentric
Tropical
Placidus
Mean Node

4. Walking into the heart of the unknown (Sun in Leo, less than two degrees from the 12th house cusp and in the same sign as it, squares the Moon in Taurus 9th house). This part of Angela also emphasises her aptitude for studying and teaching (Moon in the 9th house ruling the 11th house), this time as a lifelong and practical path towards understanding who she is in the world (fixed square to the Sun) in the face of a lost or weakened father figure (Sun close to the 12th house cusp and ruling the 12th house). In this way she encounters her own spiritual journey of appreciation for what is common to all humanity. This loss motif in her chart suggests that her family carries a theme of the weakened or absent male that goes back many generations.

◈ **What might I expect to see in her handwriting?** Her handwriting may show her practical pronoun 'I' written with serifs indicating clarity and confidence, or else quite large to compensate for insecurity. It may contain letters with undulations, indicating her aptitude to reach out to others in a teaching capacity.

5. Dependence versus independence (North Node in Pisces in the 7th house – South Node in Virgo in the 1st house conjunct Venus). This journey takes Angela into a committed relationship in her twenties (North Node in the 7th house), seeking a connection that allows her to merge deeply with another (North Node in Pisces). She may even seek a guru-type figure (dispositor is Jupiter which opposes Neptune and connects with the T-Square) only to find a sense of inadequacy, loss or disappointment. This then forces her to explore her own independence (South Node in the 1st house) and in so doing, she comes to appreciate not only her attention to detail (South Node in Virgo) and her focused mind (dispositor of South Node is Mercury conjunct Pluto) but also that she seeks connections with others that are different and alternative (South Node conjunct Venus, Venus in fall).

◈   **What might I expect to see in her handwriting?** Her handwriting may have wide margins all the way around showing independence (South Node-Venus in the 1st house). She may also use an upright script and one that contains angles (South Node in Virgo).

Here is Angela's handwriting:

I sat with my father, both wondrous beings of Light. I felt his positive qualities, warmth, humour & his desire to give me the best education. I embraced

Angela's handwriting is large and flamboyant (Mercury in Leo prominent on the Ascendant). She begins at the top of the page indicating ease and intimacy with the recipient. The handwriting has an even quality to it, with letters that sit mostly in the practical plains landscape (Moon in Taurus). They are written in an upright fashion displaying independence (South Node-Venus in the 1st house) and the lines are slanted slightly upward showing optimism (Mercury-Pluto in Leo). As well, her personal pronoun 'I' is narrow and simple, suggesting that she wants to be seen as who she is without affectation. Her letters contain some angularity, suggestive of an intellectual approach to life (Virgo Ascendant) combined with undulating letters that reach out to others, indicative of her teaching ability (Jupiter-Neptune/Moon in the 9th house).

However, there are no gestures on her letters 'f', 'h', 'l' that sweep her up into the mountains of her life. Considering that her Sun is effectively a 12th house Sun ruling the 12th house, this tells of fear around this part of her chart, suggesting that she prefers to remain in the practical realm where she can control her world.

As well, the valley loops on her letters 'g' and 'y' touch the mountain landscape of the letters below and draw to the left, suggesting she is being pulled back into the past. This sense of the past is emphasized by a decreasing left margin, lines of handwriting that gradually move closer together the further down the page she writes, and hidden luggage in her letters 'a' and 's'. Her letter 't' shows a mixture of styles, with some being capped at the top of the stem ('father'), some drawn only to the right ('Light', 'qualities', 'warmth') and others written low on the stem ('felt', 'to', 'Nanette'), showing an erratic quality to achievement and success (unaspected Saturn in the 2nd house). Considering she is writing about a meditation involving her father who died when she was sixteen, her handwriting is reflective of her process and experience.

Angela's chart contains a number of aspects which suggest difficult inherited issues from her family's past:

(i)   The Sun effectively in the 12th house ruling the 12th house: the lost, weakened or mythic father-figure.

(ii) Pluto in the 12th house connected to the 4th house: the fear of death, violence and loss of control.

(iii) Venus in Virgo (fall) in the 1st house ruling the 2nd and 10th houses: her pattern of social networking is connected with her ability to make money (2nd house) and her career (10th house). It is, however, hampered by being in fall and conjunct the South Node.

(iv) Unaspected Saturn in the 2nd house involving the 5th and 6th houses: the erratic nature of personal resources.

With her Secondary Progressed Moon moving over her MC in 2007 and transiting Saturn conjunct Pluto as transiting Pluto squares Saturn, this was a year when Angela needed to take on a large project on which she could work extremely hard as a way of soaking up the attrition and possible lack of resources (Saturn-Pluto) and in so doing gain the potential changes to her career and social status (Secondary Progressed Moon MC). Saturn was currently transiting through her 12th house and would emerge over her Ascendant in September 2007. This was the time when the hard work she had been doing behind the scenes would become visible. Since

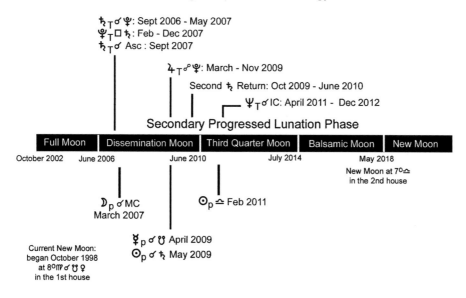

101

Saturn was natally unaspected in her 2nd house, I suggested that Angela (i) write her personal pronoun 'I' with serifs to strengthen her identity and (ii) slowly bring in her left hand margins, in order to work with her fear of the future.

What happened to Angela?

In August 2007 Angela emailed me the following:

> I was listening to your tape on my way to London the other week and something you said leapt out at me. You mentioned how important it was for me to get into my creative side and that one way of working with my chart this year would be to write a book. Well, in March I was approached by an independent UK publisher to write a Life Coaching book and I have just finished it – publication date mid-December 2007. It was a huge learning curve for me as I am relatively new to Life Coaching and the deadline was very tight.

In December 2007 Angela emailed me again:

> A year has passed since my consultation with you and I thought I'd send you the cover of my new book which is about to be published. I've also been asked by the same publishers to write another one on relationships to be published in October 2008. So it seems that this is the creative expression that you spoke about in my reading! It feels good to be doing this and fulfilling my desire to be more out in the world.

I asked Angela if she would send me another sample of her handwriting so I could see the changes. She wrote the same paragraph as she had written in September 2006:

I sat with my father, both wondrous beings of light. I felt his positive qualities – warmth, humour and his desire to give me the best

Angela's personal pronoun 'I' was now much bigger than previously and contained serifs. The direction of her letter 't' bar tilted upwards indicating enthusiasm and optimism and most of them were written to the right of the 't' stem, showing an ability to complete projects. The letter 'n' of 'education' still contained a long flourish, suggesting pride in her creativity (Mercury in Leo). Overall the writing was heavier in pressure, indicating an improved strength of will and energy, and larger than previously, indicating generosity and enthusiasm. The 'i' dots continued to be dashes or hooks in part and the letter 'o' remained open but there was far less hidden luggage in the letters 'a' and 's'.

Angela's writing now indicated a far greater confidence in herself and her place in the world. However, where before her handwriting showed a decreasing left margin, now it firmly hugged that left hand side of the page, suggesting that success had brought with it a tremendous fear of letting go of the past, and she was now holding onto it for security and solutions. Fears stem from experiences in early life. Her writing about a healing meditation concerning her father who died when she was sixteen contained the message that it was clearly still an unresolved issue.

What can Angela do?

In 2009 her Secondary Progressed Moon continues to move through the 10th house of her chart in its Disseminating phase of teaching and synthesising. In this year her Secondary Progressed Mercury conjuncts the South Node (insights, discussion and communication about past family issues or with someone from her past) as her Secondary Progressed Sun conjuncts Saturn (taking on new responsibility). She also gains a greater field of influence (transiting Jupiter opposition Pluto) as a prelude to her Second Saturn Return in October 2009.

To help Angela feel more self-assured, she could begin to move the left hand margin of her handwriting to the right, slightly at first, and then further and further over a period of six months until she felt comfortable with a wide left hand margin. She could also begin to cross her letter 't' on both sides of the stem and at the top, still with an upward slant. She might also want to put mountain sweeps on her letters 'h', 'k' and 'l' as a way of reaching the mythic inspirational father figure within her. As she instigates this next set of changes in her handwriting, she may feel resistance and she can use these feelings, images, sounds and/or insights to better understand why she is so fearful of moving ahead in her life. As well, given that this is a fertile time for her with her writing and publishing, and when her hard work and creativity are producing money and resources (unaspected Saturn in her 2nd house connected with the 5th and 6th houses), she can use this period to anchor her skills and ability to enable her to use her Saturn at will in the future instead of feeling abandoned when she cannot readily access it (the on-again/off -again quality of an unaspected planet).

As Angela makes these changes in her handwriting in conjunction with her predictive work so she helps co-create her future, and in this way her 'netivot' become visible.

7

Live with Enthusiasm

This chapter continues the task of showing you how to work with a person's chart, their handwriting and their predictive work. In order to make a comparison of a common text across many hands and demonstrate how handwriting is a function and expression of each natal chart and as such can be used with a person's predictive work to help shape their future, I requested volunteers from my students at Astro Logos. I asked them to send me two samples of their handwriting: the first was a piece written specifically for me, copying an excerpt from Samuel Ullman's book *From The Summit of Years Four Score*.[1] This would act as a control. The second was an example of their handwriting written prior to my request. I chose the piece by Ullman deliberately because what we write determines how we write it. Whilst other factors, such as how we are feeling at the time and the circumstances in which we write – where we are, the time of day, the constraints of work or family, and so on – also come into play, nevertheless the piece by Ullman (1840-1924), an American businessman, poet, humanitarian and lay rabbi, is particularly inspiring. The students were at liberty to write in any colour ink, use any type of pen and select any style or colour of paper.

---

1. Armbrester, Margaret England and Miyazawa, Jiro M. *Samuel Ullman and 'Youth': The Life, the Legacy* (Tuscaloosa: University of Alabama Press 1993).

Live with Enthusiasm

by Samuel Ullman

Youth is not a time of life. It's a state of mind. It is a temper of the will, a quality of the imagination, a vigour of the emotions, a predominance of courage over timidity, of the appetite for adventure over love of ease.

Nobody grows old by merely living a number of years. People grow old only by deserting their ideals. Years wrinkle the skin, but to give up enthusiasm wrinkles the soul.

Whether 60 or 16, there is in every being's heart the love of wonder, the sweet amazement at the stars and starlike things and thoughts, the undaunted challenge of events, the unfailing childlike appetite for what-next, and the joy in the game of living.

You are as young as your faith, as old as your doubt; as young as your self-confidence, as old as your fear; as young as your hope, as old as your despair.

So long as your heart receives messages of beauty, hope, cheer, courage, grandeur and power from the earth, from men and from the Infinite, so long are you young.

Live every day of your life as if you expect to live forever.

A note regarding my use of predictive work. In order to see the future pattern more clearly, in this chapter I have limited my tools of prediction to the Secondary Progressed Lunation cycle and to major transits. This eliminates any 'noise' and allows the overall shape to emerge. As well, whilst I have indicated letter shapes that can be undertaken to assist the changes suggested by the predictive work, a person will make changes to their handwriting that are consistent with the framework of their perception. Otherwise all of us would end up writing in exactly the same way, without distinctive characteristics that define and individualize us.

How 'Elaine' views enthusiasm

Youth is not a time of life. It is a state of mind. It is a temper of the will, a quality of the imagination, a vigour of the emotions, a predominance of courage over timidity, of the appetite for adventure over love of ease.

Nobody grows old by merely living a number of years. People grow old only by deserting their ideals. Years wrinkle the skin, but to give up enthusiasm wrinkles the soul.

Whether 60 or 16, there is in every being's heart the love of wonder, the sweet amazement at the stars and star-like things and thoughts, the undaunted challenge of events, the unfailing childlike appetite for what-next, and the joy in the game of living.

You are as young as your faith, as old as your doubt; as young as your self confidence, as old as your fear; as young as your hope, as old as your despair.

So long as your heart receives messages of beauty, hope, cheer, grandeur and power from the earth, from men and from the Infinite, so long are you young

Live everyday of your life as you expect to live forever.

Youth is not a time of life. It is a state of mind. It is a temper of the will, a quality of the imagination, a vigour of the emotions, a predominance of courage over timidity, of the appetite for adventure over love of ease.

Elaine's handwriting pattern is regular and even and sits predominantly in her practical plains landscape, suggesting that she approaches her daily world with a consistent and measured tread. Her margins are balanced on either side of the page, implying that she moves easily towards new ideas and thoughts and appears happy to leave the past behind her. However, her zig-zag left margin suggests caution and a desire to control an impulsive nature, wanting to move forward but pulled back to the past.

Her letters create undulating, friendly writing, signifying a desire to reach out to other people. There is separation and legibility in her letters, indicative of clear thinking and an ability to organize and balance her life. She also makes a ligature with her 'th' indicating flexibility in her thinking.

However, certain letters show that she is fearful of her personal creativity and holds herself back. This occurs in the tightly cemented arches of the letters 'h', 'm', 'n' and 'y', leaving no air in between.

Her letters lean towards the right, revealing someone who is sociable and emotionally outgoing, thus well-suited to working with people. However, this can also suggest impatience, a more likely expression given the zig-zag margin with its self-regulating shape pulling back on over-eagerness. As well, some of her letters sweeping down into the valleys fuse with the mountains of the line below, implying that she may at times be intolerant and lack diplomacy. Together with the cemented arches, this implies that her natural inquisitiveness was squashed by a parent who also instilled in her a fear of self-expression. This is reinforced by the low 't' bars in the plains landscape crossed horizontally and level, suggesting that she keeps her goals low in order to readily achieve them, rather than stretching to achieve goals that may at first appear beyond her grasp but which would ultimately give her greater satisfaction. Indeed many of her 't' letters extend down into the valleys, suggesting a lack of belief in her own ability to achieve things for herself. Reinforcing this is the fact that her letter 'f' often contains a lower loop only, suggesting she is fearful of her own ideas and plans, and that she avoids focusing too much attention on her goals and dreams. Additionally Elaine adds skipping ropes or trails to the left of her letters at the beginning of some words, showing that she needs a great deal of inner preparation before beginning a task.

Finally Elaine forms her capital 'I' like the letter 'l'. Written as a complete loop, this suggests that when it comes to self-definition there are issues she wants to control or hide.

How Elaine's chart speaks to her through her handwriting

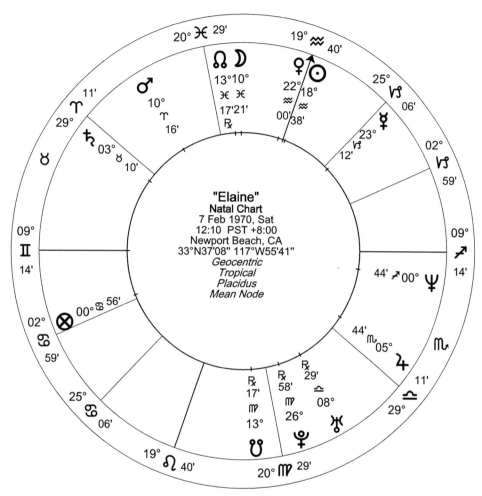

What parts of Elaine's chart indicate her fear of personal creativity and hence hold her back?

1. The first way is by being placed in the public eye where Elaine achieves emotional satisfaction either as a healer or carer (Moon in Pisces in the 10th house conjunct the North Node). Elaine has learnt from her mother how to seek emotional oneness with another via a spiritual or healing expression, through the arts, or simply through being a mother herself. This is something that she values (ruling the 2nd house) and which gives her a voice (ruling the 3rd house). Yet in so doing she has to learn how to handle feeling overwhelmed by other people's emotions (Moon in Pisces, Moon trine Jupiter) and so will often seek seclusion as

a way of re-establishing her emotional centre of gravity. This presents her with a dichotomy: wanting the emotional satisfaction of public acclaim and wanting seclusion.

2. The second way is in learning from her partner how to maintain clear boundaries when handling groups of people who daily flood her life (Neptune in the 6th house affinity 11th house). This pattern may first have been modeled by a parent (Neptune making a wide conjunction to the Descendant) who chose illness or tiredness as a way of gaining space and separation from others. However, its best expression is in the form of work that involves imagination, the fine arts or therapeutic skills.

3. The third way is through an immense drive for creative freedom, both in working with groups and on her own (Mars in rulership opposition Uranus across the 5th-11th axis).

How does Elaine's chart show her lack of self-belief and inability to achieve things for herself?

Elaine's chart contains ambition and the accompanying desire for status and recognition (Sun-Venus in Aquarius conjunct the MC). However, the journey of the 10th house Sun which is modeled by the father-figure takes many years to achieve and may meanwhile be projected onto other solar figures in her world including her partner, allowing them to achieve whilst she supports them as the nurturer and carer (Moon in Pisces in the 10th house).

In terms of her communication (unaspected duet of Mercury in Capricorn trine Pluto), there may have been an early obstruction to her thinking (Mercury in Capricorn) resulting in worry or concern (Mercury-Pluto) which compelled her to pay attention to how she thought, wrote and spoke with others. In its best expression this can produce an intense and focused communicator (Mercury-Pluto) who can formulate and frame her ideas (Mercury in Capricorn). However, the unaspected quality of this trine means it has an on again-off again characteristic and unless Elaine can build a bridge between the two feeling states in order to access her incisive communication skills at will, she may never feel entirely sure that she has the ability to communicate effectively.

What part of her chart designates Elaine's impatience and lack of diplomacy?

Both her Mars-Uranus and her Mercury-Pluto can hinder her diplomacy.

Elaine's background

I am a 38 year old stay-at-home mom, happily married for nine years with two boys ages six years and two years. I was adopted at birth, am left-handed, and went away from home to university at eighteen years, and studied both business and teaching primary age children. I taught various ages for about ten years before having a baby at thirty-two and deciding to stay home until my children left 'the nest'. I love 'traditional' activities like cooking, quilting, sewing, and gardening, but think of myself as unconventional. My friends would describe me as a good listener, but opinionated. I want to find a way to combine my love for textiles, teaching, and even a talent for counseling others into a career that will allow me to have some freedom to modify it to my life as it evolves. I also feel that it is important that I focus now on raising my boys responsibly, helping them to mature and be good citizens. My husband and I are agreed on this but can hardly wait until it is just the two of us again (smile).

Elaine's predictive astrology

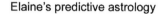

♃ᴛ♂ ☉/MC/♀
April - December 2009

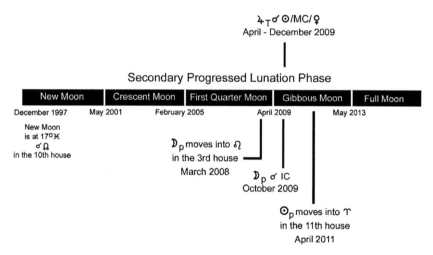

What can Elaine do to help co-create her 'netivot'?

In Elaine's predictive work, her Secondary Progressed Moon moves into Leo in March 2008, a time when she engages with a stronger sense of her own creativity. In late October 2009 her Secondary Progressed Moon crosses the IC whilst transiting Jupiter sweeps across her Sun-MC-Venus, suggesting both an expansion of her outer world and the establishment of a more secure base from which to operate. In 2011 her Secondary Progressed Sun changes sign from Pisces to Aries in the 11th house, a year that will usher in a far more independent path for her, allowing her to implement new ways of interacting with or leading groups. So Elaine's opportunity to combine her love for textiles, teaching, and counseling others as a career in later life may be approaching sooner than she thinks. In order to encourage that pathway, she can slowly bring the following changes into her handwriting:

1. She can begin to loosen the cemented arches of her letters 'h', 'm', 'n' and 'y' to help her let go of old patterns that are inhibiting her from taking the next steps forward and gain greater confidence in her abilities.

   temper   m   n   h   y

2. She can change her capital 'I' to one that redefines her sense of self in the world.

   cli   I

3. She can raise the cross bar on the 't' to the top and angle it upwards to focus her goals, and carry the base of her 't' forward in order to make sure that it does not extend down into her valley landscape.

   state   t

4. She can give more space between the lines so that the valley loops of her 'y' letters do not crash into the mountains below.

   *timidity,
   over love*

5. She can change her 'f' to a 'bow and arrow' 'f' so that it contains all three landscapes.

   confidence   f

As Elaine begins to make these changes to her handwriting, events will occur in her external world to both support and undermine the way she wants to feel and be in the world, so she must be prepared to follow through with what is offered to her to help manifest her goals. In combination with her predictive work, she can then work towards achieving them.

How 'Charlotte' views enthusiasm

Youth is not a time of life. It's a state of mind. It is a temper of the will, a quality of the imagination, a vigour of the emotions, a predominance of courage over timidity, of the appetite for adventure over love of ease.

Nobody grows old by merely living a number of years. People grow old only by deserting their ideals. Years wrinkle the skin, but to give up enthusiasm wrinkles the soul.

Whether 60 or 16, there is in every being's heart the love of wonder, the sweet amazement at the stars and starlike things and thoughts, the undaunted challenge of events, the unfailing childlike appetite for what-next, and the joy in the game of living.

You are as young as your faith, as old as your doubt; as young as your self-confidence, as old as your fear; as young as your hope, as old as your despair.

So long as your heart receives messages of beauty, hope, cheer, courage, grandeur and power from the earth, from men and from the Infinite, so long are you young.

Live every day of your life as if you expect to live forever.

Youth is not a time of life. It's a state of mind. It is a temper of the will, a quality of the imagination, a vigour of the emotions, a predominance of courage over timidity, of the appetite for adventure over love of ease.

Charlotte writes on lined paper where the left hand margin has been imprinted by the manufacturer. Her handwriting is mainly focused in the practical landscape and in this there is a mix of styles. Her letters slant to the right, indicating the desire to reach out to others and seek friendship and company. Indeed dominating her handwriting are the undulating shapes of friendly writing representative of the need to relate, socialize and share thoughts and ideas. However, her handwriting hugs the imprinted left hand margin tightly, suggesting that she is fearful of the future, and that when it comes to planning, she prefers to accept other people's suggestions. She also writes exactly on the lines, suggesting that she feels more at ease in a practical world where there are frameworks and scaffolding, preferring to follow orders rather than make her own decisions. Like a child holding onto the side of the swimming pool who longs to swim out to the deep end with the rest, this presents her with a dilemma.

Her 'i' dots are made to the right of the letter and are generally dashes or hooks. An 'i' dot placed to the right of the letter indicates that Charlotte is future-orientated, enthusiastic and often impulsive. However, she may also be so caught in the hopes of what might occur that she hasn't yet put her ideas into place. Several valley loops on her letter 'y' tangle with the mountain landscape below, signifying impatience. Her letters 'm', 'n', 'h' are often angular, indicating that she is in part driven by inner tension and uses her intellect as a way of handling her emotions.

Charlotte also writes her 't' letters in two separate ways, yet both ways have the 't' bar sitting low in the practical plains landscape, suggesting that she sets her goals only so high as she feels she can comfortably accomplish from what she knows already, rather than stretching to manifest her dreams. Often the 't' bar is written to the right of the letter, pointing to the fact that she prefers to complete projects rather initiate them. Additionally her 't' is full of hidden luggage, an extra loop made on the lower right side as she pulls her pen back to the letter stem to make the cross bar. This suggests that there is a lake of trapped ideas, possibly quite unconscious, connected with what she wants to achieve for herself that she is fearful of divulging. Further, her letter 'd' on three occasions ('mind', 'undaunted', and 'and' in the second last paragraph) is written with a ballooning stem in the mountain landscape, indicative of an underlying sense of helplessness, a sensitivity to what people say about her and a consequent fear of confrontation. There are also secrets she feels the need to hide from other people, revealed in the hidden luggage made in her letter 'o'. In some cases where the 'o' is completely encircled, these are secrets that are metaphorically strangling her.

Charlotte writes her letter 'b' open to left and often with container at bottom, like a large hanging wire with a hook. Whilst the shape of the letter drives forward, the letter is both open on the left hand side suggesting a place where information from her past escapes, and a concealed container at the letter's base suggesting a secret she carries which stifles her expression.

Finally, Charlotte writes her letter 'f' sweeping up into her mountain landscape, showing that she has dreams and goals. However, what supports them is a thin fishing line into the valleys of her emotions. Charlotte has great hopes and ideas but feels she has no ability to manifest them in the practical world.

Indeed her handwriting shows that few of her dreams are allowed to rise above the parapet of practicality.

How Charlotte's chart speaks to her through her handwriting

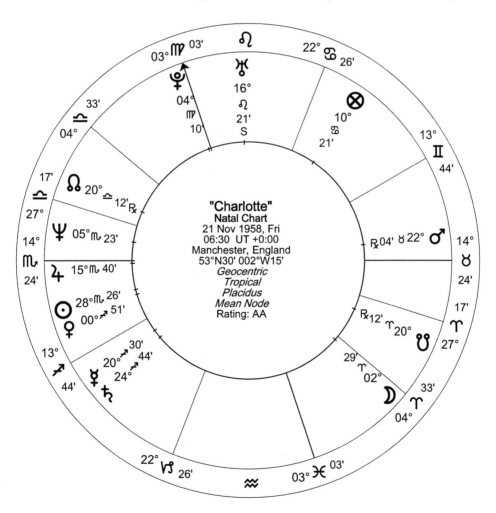

What parts of Charlotte's chart suggest her fear of achievement and success?

1. The first part describes a conditional parent whom Charlotte saw as powerful and who has become the role model, for better or for worse, for how Charlotte is to be in the world (Pluto conjunct the MC). Such a path involves at its heart issues of trust and betrayal where loyalty and commitment (Pluto square Venus) struggle with freedom and independence (Venus in Sagittarius). For a small child such intensity can prove frightening and overwhelming. It could take many years for Charlotte to recognize that she can work with these energies in her career.

2. The second part is modeled for her by her father-figure (Sun) whom she sees as possessing a natural sense of leadership and authority (Sun in 1st house) through connections of blood and/or allegiance (Sun in Scorpio) and driven by business or personal commitments (Sun in 1st house opposition Mars in the 7th house). Being the path of her Sun, it can take until her mid-to-late-thirties for her to begin to feel comfortable with such a position in her world. It may be easier to project these parts of her chart onto other solar heroes such as a business partner or an intimate relationship.

3. The third part describes a problem-solving tool in Charlotte's chart (Jupiter-Mars-Uranus T-Square). Whilst she is seen as someone who is bountiful, confident and gregarious (Jupiter conjunct the Ascendant) and who values and grows from self-knowledge (Jupiter ruling the 2nd house) and relies on it as a foundation stone (Jupiter ruling the 4th house), she is at the same time dependent upon a personal or business partner to motivate her (Mars in 7th house ruling the 1st and 6th houses and in opposition to Jupiter) in ways that are different to or at odds with the mainstream (Mars in detriment). She can solve this dilemma between dependence and independence (1st-7th houses axis) slowly, practically and one step at a time (fixed T-Square) through education and/or travel, and by encounters with philosophies which are different or unique (Uranus as the apex planet of the T-Square). However, as she does so, she is forced to take risks (Jupiter square Uranus) and to learn to handle an immense drive (Mars-Uranus) through patience and pacing (Mars in Taurus).

What parts of Charlotte's chart contain hidden family issues?
In Charlotte's family there is an unconscious issue regarding loss and confusion that has been in her family for many generations (Neptune in 12th house makes a wide conjunction to the Ascendant and in the same sign as the Ascendant. Additionally, it is a planet in the 12th house which is also the ruler of the 4th

house, embedding the inherited family issue even more strongly). This may have been expressed by members of her family in previous generations as a loss of physical or mental capabilities or loss of home and subsequent exile. Rather than act as the unconscious servant or victim of her family's unexpressed concerns. Charlotte's rite of passage is to have faith in her own spirituality separate to that of her family.

Charlotte's background

I was born in England, the eldest of three children. My family emigrated in 1967 to the USA and we moved again to Canada in 1980. I trained as a physiotherapist, married my husband and then worked until I gave birth to my first of five children in 1987. Since then I have been a stay-at-home mum. As my children have aged, I became interested in astrology and over the last few years I have been studying and working towards earning my qualifications.

Growing up in another country can be a difficult experience for a young child and as a result one tends to feel off balance for years. Therefore I hope with age and maturity to find the confidence to express myself in an authentic fashion and feel fulfilled and worthwhile on a level that goes beyond my identity as a mother.

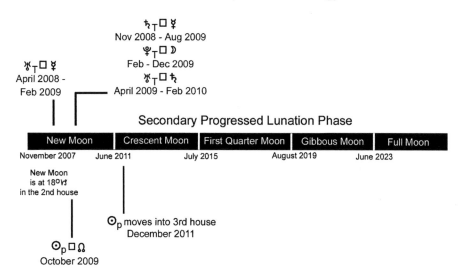

Charlotte's predictive astrology

What can Charlotte do to help co-create her 'netivot'?

In late 2007 Charlotte moved into a new Secondary Progressed New Moon Lunation phase, so she is in the phase of planting, sowing Capricorn seeds in her 2nd house. Now is the time for her to forge new pathways of responsibility built on a solid sense of self-worth and self-esteem.

Her transits in 2008 indicate that this is a fertile period for new thinking (transiting Uranus square Mercury) followed by a period of consolidating those ideas in 2009 (transiting Saturn square Mercury/transiting Uranus square Saturn). Amongst this is a great deal of emotional stress connected with her own mother or her role as a mother (transiting Pluto square the Moon), such as the first child leaving home. As well, in late 2009 her progressed Sun squares the nodal axis, placing her ego, identity and vitality under stress. In late 2011, her progressed Sun moves into her 3rd house, reinforcing the focus on new learning and communication skills.

In order to encourage the path she wants for herself and in tandem with her predictive work, Charlotte can slowly begin to bring the following changes into her handwriting:

1. She can begin to write on lined paper without an imprinted left margin and as she becomes confident in forming her own margins, she can begin writing on unlined paper.

2. She can pay attention to how she dots her letter 'i', placing it directly above the stem.

3. She can reshape her letters 'b', 'd', and 'o' so that they no longer contain any unwanted luggage.

4. She can reshape her letter 't' to eliminate unwanted luggage and raise the cross bar to the top of the letter, made evenly from left to right and angled slightly upward, to help her set and achieve her goals.

emobins $\mathcal{T}$

5. She can consciously make sweeps up into her mountain landscape with clear loops on her letters 'h', 'k' and 'l', emphasizing the goals she wants to achieve.

enthusiasm crinkles
h k l

6. She can begin to make a 'bow-and-arrow' letter 'f' to make sure that her dreams have a chance of manifesting.

of   *f*

However, as Charlotte makes these changes to her handwriting – slowly and only one at a time until she feels comfortable with each of them – she must be prepared to handle and act on the changes that will take place in her life.

How 'Patricia' views enthusiasm

Youth is not a time of life. It's a state of mind.
It is a temper of the will, a quality of the imagination,
a vigour of the emotions, a predominence of courage
over timidity, of the appetite for adventure over
love of ease.

Nobody grows old by merely living a number of years.
People grow old only by deserting their ideals.
Years wrinkle the skin, but to give up enthusiasm
wrinkles the soul.

Whether 60 or 16, there is in every being's heart the
love of wonder, the sweet amazement at the stars and
starlike things and thoughts, the undaunted
challenge of events, the unfailing childlike appetite
for what-next, and the joy in the game of living.

You are as young as your faith, as old as your
doubt; as young as your self-confidence, as old as
your fear; as young as your hope, as old as your
despair.

So long as your heart receives messages of beauty,
hope, cheer, courage, grandeur and power from
the earth, from men and from the Infinite, so long
are you young.
Live every day of your life as if you expect to live forever.

Youth is not a time of life. It's a state of mind..
It is a temper of the will, a quality of the imagination,
a vigour of the emotions, a predominence of courage
over timidity, of the appetite for adventure over
love of ease.

Patricia chose to write on unlined pale green paper, suggesting solitude and peacefulness. Her handwriting maintains a relatively wide left margin indicating a balanced attitude to the past, aware of it and happy to leave it where it is and move forward with life, and the consistently straight left margin suggests a disciplined mind. As well, whilst her first line of writing follows a relatively horizontal line, the further down the page she writes, the more the lines begin to rise upward. This indicates optimism and enthusiasm, someone who is happy to work hard and has a strong desire for self-expression. The spacing between her words and between her lines is even, indicative of an organized mind, and Patricia's letters are written predominantly with an upright vertical script pointing towards a strong sense of independence. However, dominating Patricia's handwriting are the long lower loops of her letters 'f', 'g', 'p', 'q' 'y' and 'z' which flood deeply into her valley landscape, indicative of emotional or even sexual issues. The fact that these crash into the mountains of the lines below suggests that these emotions overpower her thoughts. Her capital 'I' is written with a full loop in the mountain landscape. As well, Patricia writes her letter 'p' with a large loop to the left of the stem which pours into her valley landscape. The art she creates with this letter is of a someone who lugs an extremely large pack on their back, full of old emotional issues connected with the past, and who has never given herself permission to speak about the issues or to confront those who originated the distress.

Often Patricia writes her 'th' as a ligature, representative of a fluid thinker. However, amongst the verticality, she writes her letters 'b', 'f', 'g', 'p,' and 'y' with a leftward slant, demonstrating a desire to withdraw from the world. Her letter 'g', written as a figure eight, shows creativity, yet the introductory stroke is an enclosing circle, suggesting that Patricia holds on tightly to a secret about her past, fearful that someone will find out about it.

Patricia's letter 'f' begins with a single line thrust into her mountain landscape and a full loop ballooning into her valley landscape which she then completes by pulling to the left. The image she creates with this letter is of a periscope peering up to the mountains to look in awe and wonder at what might be but which is so weighted with emotional ballast it pulls her down below the surface of life. The backward flick indicates the emotions that involuntarily pull her back to the past. This is someone who has let their ideas be shaped so much by others for reasons of necessity that she now feels unable to manifest any dreams of her own, and thus can only view them with despair. Her letter 'd' contains a large loop in the stem sweeping up into her mountain landscape, suggesting someone who interprets the world rather than understands it and hence takes things personally, often blaming others and refusing to confront people and deal with situations as they occur. This is combined with 'i' dots which are mostly hooks, indicating resentment, several 't' bars that slope downwards ('temper', 'imagination', 'emotions', 'appetite', 'starlike') indicating closed ideas, and a 't' that is often joined with the 'i' next to it obliterating the 'i' (a word pun on 'eye' and seeing clearly). All together these indicate someone who has previously had to dance to another's tune, and who as a result is now tightly and rigidly controlling their own world.

Yet in many areas Patricia's handwriting shows that she does have goals she wants to achieve: often she writes her letter 't' with a cross bar relatively high up the 't' stem and balanced; her letter 'l' arcs up into the mountain landscape towards her goals, expressed in words like 'will', 'challenge', 'quality' and 'childlike'; and her letters 'g', 'y' and 'z' most of the time complete to the right.

Overall this is the handwriting of someone who is caught in a double-bind, someone who is practically focused, who can achieve other people's goals but whose own dreams have been eroded by time and necessity and lie unfulfilled, unconsciously covered with resentment and despair.

Patricia's spontaneous handwriting

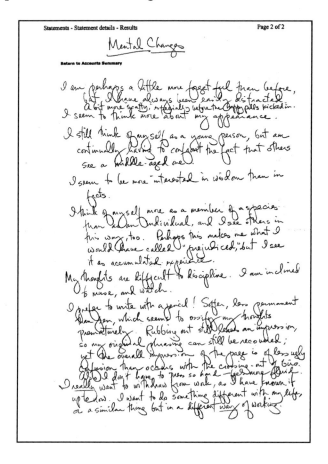

In this handwriting Patricia reveals more clues which underpin her state of mind. Written in pencil, it contains a zig-zag margin indicating the desire to move away from the past which she then corrects with each new thought. She writes:

My thoughts are difficult to discipline. I am inclined to muse and watch. I prefer to write with a pencil! Softer, less permanent than pen, which seems to ossify my thoughts prematurely. Rubbing out still leaves an impression, so my original phrasing can still be recorded; yet the overall impression of the page is of less ugly confusion than occurs with the crossing-out of biro. Also I don't have to press so hard – feels more fluid. I really want to withdraw from work, as I have known it up to now. I want to do something different with my life, or a simliar thing but in a different way of working.

How Patricia's chart speaks to her through her handwriting

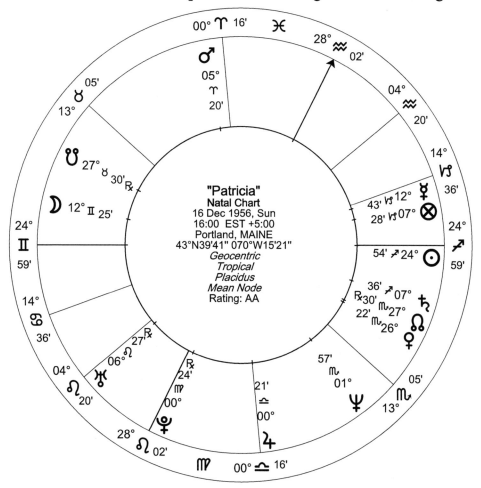

What parts of Patricia's chart contain issues from the past that may still have a hold over her?

1. The first part describes a deep bond with her mother that also contains issues of abandonment, loss and separation anxiety (Moon in the 12th house in Gemini opposition Saturn in the 6th house), connected to an early deprivation of resources (2nd-8th resource axis brought in by rulership of the Moon and Saturn).

2. The second part describes a family pattern of rigidity and obstinacy (South Node in Taurus in the 12th house) where a refusal to handle intense emotions has meant family members have held grudges against each other, resulting in family feuds. (South Node disposed by an unaspected Venus in Scorpio in detriment in the 6th house conjunct the North Node).

3. The third part describes an intense childhood filled with passionate adult emotions, such as death, sexuality or aggression (Pluto conjunct the IC with an affinity to the 6th house square Saturn in the 6th house ruling the 8th and, by old rulerships, the 9th houses) and which may be part of a family pattern of intensity and violence.

How does Patricia's chart show her lack of self-belief?

1. Patricia will feel, throughout her life, drawn towards and compelled to be in relationships, either intimate or business, as a way of defining herself (the Sun makes a partile conjunction to the Descendant) and gaining her voice (Sun rules the 3rd house). This is a complex double-edged sword, for the path of her Sun is at once one of freedom and independence (Sun in Sagittarius) and one of commitment (Sun conjunct the Descendant). As well, since the Sun makes no aspect to any planet or luminary, it is also one where she either feels strongly defined when in partnership or has no sense of herself at all (the on-again/off-again quality of an unaspected luminary). Until she learns to appreciate that being in relationship is her only way of gaining her freedom, and until she is able to recognize that through her partner she discovers her own solar strength, she may find it hard to achieve the identity she seeks in her life.

2. Patricia is seen as someone with a tremendous drive to express herself (Gemini Ascendant, ruler Mercury square to Mars) through groups (Mars in the 11th) and working with other people's resources (Mercury within two degrees of the 8th house cusp and in the same sign). However, whilst she thinks slowly and practically and likes to see concrete results from her ideas (Mercury in Capricorn), her knowledge base and thus how she interacts with groups are continually

undergoing change and upheaval (Mercury within two degrees of the 8th house cusp and in the same sign). Yet as she struggles with her thinking and the way she structures and expresses herself, so she finds inspiration and an ability to work long and hard on projects she loves (Mars in rulership in Aries in the 11th house forming a Grand Trine in fire with Saturn in the 6th house and Uranus in the 3rd house). If she is not involved in fertilizing her own ideas, she may find this inherent talent (Grand Trine) being leached away from her, unable to build on opportunities as they arise.

3. As Patricia reaches her early-to-mid twenties, she encounters what she feels is a rewarding daily working life (the North Node), filled with relationships that are intense, passionate and monogamous (Venus in Scorpio in the 6th house conjunct the North Node). However, whilst this may initially be successful, towards her late twenties Patricia finds she has to handle instead issues of trust and betrayal and is then forced, consciously or unconsciously, first to seek the stability and steadiness of her own family (South Node in Taurus in the 12th house) and then later that of large organizations in order to allow her to re-encounter intensity in relationships once she has gained maturity (Venus in Scorpio in the 6th house conjunct the North Node). In this way she is better able understand the nature of passion in her social networks and gain a more three-dimensional fulfilment of it in her daily life.

Patricia's background

I grew up in Scarborough, Maine, USA. My father's family caught and sold lobsters, fish, shrimp and clams. My mother's family were farmers. My dad had his own business, selling seafood wholesale and retail, and my mother did his bookkeeping in an office at home. I have two brothers and two sisters, one of each older and younger than me, who still live fairly near each other in Maine. I first learned astrology there, from a friend of my aunt's.

Keen to get well away, I went to Florida to study English Literature, because Eckerd College had an extensive study abroad programme. I did two terms in London and one in Barcelona. I loved Britain and came to dread going back to the States, and in the end I married for convenience (ha!) in order to stay here. I had hoped to work in publishing, but living in Uxbridge, I ended up working in local government, where I found my way into libraries. I qualified in Birmingham, and have worked in the large central reference library there for the past twenty-four years, where I've been responsible for buying the astrology books, among other subjects.

I've found my career disappointing and increasingly frustrating, as local government has become less orientated towards providing services for the public good, and increasingly embraced a bullshitting business model. However,

I've enjoyed strong bonds of loyalty and shared yearning (for escape) with my colleagues.

I'm now working towards a combined career doing astrology and harp therapy. I don't know how it will work out, but I feel I want to organise my life around the two things I most enjoy doing, and I feel I'm embracing opportunities again, as I did when I was young. That in itself is a great joy, since for quite a few years I felt that opportunities had stopped coming my way – the river of life had changed its course and left me stranded.

I don't feel that way any more.

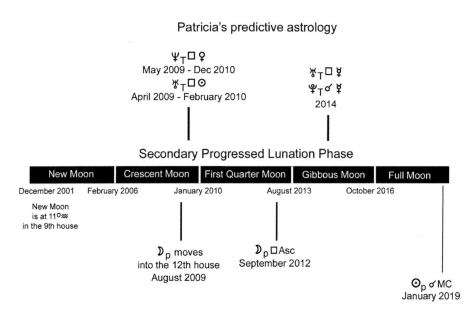

Patricia's predictive astrology

What can Patricia do to help co-create her 'netivot'?

In 2001 Patricia began a New Scondary Progressed Lunation cycle seeded at 11 degrees of Aquarius in her 9th house. So this cycle of twenty nine and a half years is concerned with travel or teaching or academic study or in some way encountering a new philosophy (9th house) that brings into play her intellect and her ideas (Aquarius). Patricia has said that she wants to work towards a combined career of astrology and harp therapy. How then can she change her handwriting to help shape her predictive work and so implement her dreams?

Firstly, in considering the astrology, in August 2009 the Secondary Progressed Moon moves into her 12th house, signalling a time of focused effort behind the scenes until September 2012 when the Secondary Progressed Moon moves over her Ascendant and the results of her hard work become visible.

In 2009, transiting Neptune squares Patricia's Venus (Romantic Love or bringing harp therapy into her life more fully) as transiting Uranus squares her

Sun (the unexpected redefinition of self). If ever there was to be a year when she could begin to redefine herself 2009 suggests itself as a likely candidate, prefacing three years of work in the background when she can slowly build a new identity. Transiting Neptune continues to square her Venus throughout 2010, emphasising this redefiniton. Looking forward in time to 2014 when she becomes visible to the world again, transiting Uranus squares her Mercury (encountering new ideas) as transiting Pluto conjuncts her Mercury (obsession with an idea and putting her energy and focus into it). If ever there was to be a year when she could begin to implement her new voice (Mercury), 2014 is surely that year. Furthermore, in January 2019 when she turns sixty-two, Patricia's Secondary Progressed Sun moves over her MC and into her 10th house, where it remains for some thirty-two years. Clearly the best years of her life, when she could potentially enjoy a fulfilling time as an astrologer/harp therapist, lie ahead of her.

Therefore, with regard to her handwriting, Patricia can slowly begin to put into practice the following changes, taking one letter at a time and working with it to fully integrate it before moving on to the next:

1. She can create a more balanced letter 'f' that accesses all three landscapes and allows her to focus on her dreams and set realistic goals for achieving them.

2. She can begin to release the heavy accumulation of blame suggested by the inflated letter 'd' stem and implement ways of confronting people and situations as they occur.

3. She can release the heavy pack of old emotional issues attached to the letter 'p'.

4. She can slowly start to raise her 't' bar to the top, rising from left to right.

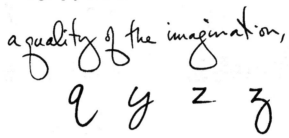

5. She can focus on creating much smaller loops in the valley landscape of her letters 'f', 'g', 'q' 'y' and 'z'.

6. She can open the top of her creative letter 'g' and help to release the fear around a secret from her past.

7. She can take care in how she makes the 'i' dots so that she slowly releases unconscious resentment and learns to actualize her dreams and goals in the present.

8. She can change her personal pronoun 'I' to one that redefines her sense of self in the world.

All of these handwriting changes will take time to implement for, as Patricia brings in each new way of shaping her letters, the course of her inner and hence outer life will alter and it will be up to her to accept the responsibility connected with what she encounters. However, the bottom line is that Patricia no longer wants the life she has now and if she truly wants a fulfilled life, and her predictive work indicates the potential for that to happen, then it is worth putting in the effort now to slowly re-navigate and co-create her path and in so doing, come to understand her own 'netivot.'

How 'Teija' views enthusiasm

Youth is not a time of life. It's a state of mind. It is a temper of the will, a quality of the imagination, a vigour of the emotions, a predominance of courage over timidity, of the appetite for adventure over love of ease.

Nobody grows old by merely living a number of years. People grow old only by deserting their ideals. Years wrinkle the skin, but to give up enthusiasm wrinkles the soul.

Whether 60 or 16, there is in every being's heart the love of wonder, the sweet amazement at the stars and starlike things and thoughts, the undaunted challenge of events, the unfailing childlike appetite for what-next, and the joy in the game of living.

You are as young as your faith, as old as your doubt; as young as your self-confidence, as old as your fear; as young as your hope, as old as your despair.

So long as your heart receives messages of beauty, hope, cheer, courage, grandeur and power from the earth, from men and from the Infinite, so long are you young.

Live every day of your life as if you expect to live forever.

Youth is not a time of life. It's a state of mind. It is a temper of the will, a quality of the imagination, a vigour of the emotions, a predominance of courage over timidity, of the appetite for adventure over love of ease.

Teija wrote her sample in blue biro on white paper. The general layout of her handwriting on the page is tidy and pleasing. She maintains a consistent left hand margin which is relatively narrow, suggesting concern at leaving the past too far behind her. She has left a wide top margin showing either respect or reserve. She leaves little or no right hand margin indicative of someone who is co-operative and gregarious, has an enthusiasm for life, and a desire to be involved with others. Her line direction is straight and horizontal, revealing someone who is reliable, methodical, responsible and with self-control. She writes with constricted spacing between individual lines indicating a scrupulous, careful attitude, yet she maintains clear spacing between each of her paragraphs, indicating someone who is concerned about her clarity of thought, guided more by reason than feelings and emotion.

The dominant characteristic of Teija's handwriting is that it is centered in the plains landscape containing immense practicality. Her handwriting is also dominated by loops in her valley landscapes that remain open and wide, indicating an affectionate nature with some emotional immaturity. Her letters are written with a vertical upright slant, indicating that she thinks before she acts and her individual letters are spacious, suggesting she is receptive to new ideas and therefore to other people, someone who participates in life with a warm-hearted genial temperament. She lifts her pen off the page regularly, allowing new ideas to percolate into her own thinking. As well, she writes her 'th' flowing together as a ligature, representative of a fluid thinker with a flexible attitude who copes well under stressful conditions. However, whether as part of the ligature or as a separate letter, Teija places the cross-bar on her letter 't' low in her practical landscape, suggesting that she sets low goals for herself. Her letters 'o' ('vigour', 'of', 'grow') and 'b' ('by', 'but', 'being's') contain hidden luggage, indicating that she keeps confidences given to her by other people which may be a burden upon her.

Teija's spontaneous handwriting

Since Teija is writing in English as her second language, I used her spontaneous handwriting detailing her biography as a comparison. It shows a much narrower left hand margin which tapers to non-existent as it reaches the bottom of the page, suggesting shyness and a desire for seclusion. There is almost no right hand margin, indicative of a zest for life and a desire to relate to others. Indeed Teija has squeezed the words 'experiences' and 'settled' into the space at the end of lines 22 and 24 above, indicating a lack of organization, and rushing in before ascertaining the lie of the land. She also writes with much tighter line spacing, indicating self-confidence and spontaneity, as well as the need for contact with others. Together

> **Short biographical information**
>
> My parents were farmers and I grew up in our farm with them and my grandmother and my little brother. Death in my family irrevocably changed the course of things and I have not continued to be a farmer. Instead learning new things, education, studying seems to be a guideline in my life. My education is Bachelor of Business Administration in the field of library and information services as well as an artisan of decorative and restoration painting. However at the moment I work as a cook in a private home for the elderly and simultaneously learn catering in an adult education center.
>
> My true passion is astrology and I've had the privilege to study this field with Astro Logos. I strongly believe I'm an astrologer in the making! I have studied some psychology and social work in the open university as well. All I really hope for the future is to find suitable tools for helping and inspiring people and thus creating new ways. Career issues are not easy, I'm hungry for life and many kind of experiences! I have never been in a relationship. I find that a bit weird, but that is just how things have settled. But I think I'm family-orientated too, but it's too soon to ponder these issues. I enjoy life walking to my own drumbeat and take life as it presents itself. I am restless and indeed interested in many, many things in life. I feel as if many options are open at this stage (and age).

her margins and line spacing reflect someone who is both hungry for life and rushes towards it, sometimes without planning, yet still reliant on or held back by the past.

Along with her 'th', Teija also writes her 'i' dots as ligatures, carrying the dot into the following letter ('things', 'Business Administration', 'library', 'suitable', 'helping') indicating a quick and agile mind with excellent powers of concentration and deduction. She writes her capital 'I' with serifs, showing clear thinking, confidence and independence. However, her letter 's' ('course', 'studying', 'seems', 'services') contains a cellar of stored issues, emotions which have crept into her practical landscape, unconsciously surrounding and isolating them for fear they will penetrate the orderliness of her practical world. Furthermore, Teija scoops up her letter 'a' ('have', 'learning', 'education') almost totally encircling it, suggesting she is hiding things about herself from others. This also occurs from time to time with the circular part of her letter 'g' ('things', 'learning', 'astrologer', 'walking'). Teija varies the form of her letter 'f' from a hook ('life', 'future') to a slender spyglass in her mountain landscape atop a stick that barely juts into her valley landscape ('farmer', 'family') to a self-sabotaging propellor 'f' ('field', 'for'), suggesting that she has goals she wants to achieve but will not allow herself to accomplish them. Connected with this is the fact that some of her letter 'i' dots are jagged, suggesting unconscious irritation.

How Teija's chart speaks to her through her handwriting

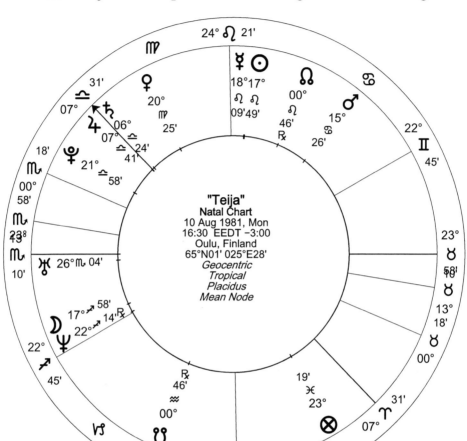

"Teija"
Natal Chart
10 Aug 1981, Mon
16:30 EEDT −3:00
Oulu, Finland
65°N01' 025°E28'
Geocentric
Tropical
Placidus
Mean Node

What parts of Teija's chart indicate a fear of emotions?

1. Teija is seen by others as unusual and independent (Uranus conjunct the Ascendant), someone who approaches life through the lens of intellect rather than emotions and who uses communication to break patterns (Uranus has an affinity with the 3rd house). This approach has been imprinted from and reinforced by her father-figure (Sun square Uranus) whom she sees as different or radical and who handles turmoil and change (Sun in the 8th house) with cool-headed reason (Sun-Uranus). Yet contained in her story is an identity caught between two grounds where Teija's overtly logical expression of self (Sun square Uranus) wrestles with her more intuitive side (Sun trine Neptune). This is her internal tussle between

physics versus metaphysics, rational versus irrational, all of which are reliant upon encounters with other cultures (the Sun rules the 9th house).

2. Teija also sees her father-figure as someone who has flashes of inspiration (Mercury-Uranus), whether or not he acts on them (the myth of the Sun in Leo is the myth of the Fisher-King who is wounded in the groin, thus Teija is somehow aware of the ways in which her father figure in her youth is wounded or powerless) and it is from him that she has inherited the trait of brilliance in her thinking, often finding that her unusual and insightful ideas come to her as complete packages (Mercury-Uranus) which she then has to unpack one step at a time (fixed square). However, once again but in a different form rests the same dilemma, for underlying this clarity of intellect is a spontaneous and highly creative talent (fire trine) for using her intuition to connect ideas. Indeed her best thinking occurs when she allows her mind to remain unfocused (Mercury trine Neptune). She can then take those ideas and shape them through logic and reason (Mercury square Uranus). If this intuitive approach is crushed by an intellect which views emotions with suspicion (Mercury-Uranus) rather than honoured as a valid way of understanding knowledge (Mercury-Neptune), Teija may experience confusion and loss in her speech, learning, ideas, and in the way she moves and walks.

3. Teija has also imprinted behaviour from her mother which encompasses similar contradictions: on the one hand an emotional sensitivity, compassion and deep intuitiveness about other people's emotional states (Moon conjunct Neptune); on the other, a desire for emotional independence and a reluctance for emotional commitment (Moon in Sagittarius), both of which impact on her self-esteem (Moon within five degrees of the 2nd house cusp and in the same sign as it) and how she handles resources, both personal and those of other people (Moon rules Cancer which is intercepted in the 8th house).

Given that her Uranus is in effect the guardian of the gate of her chart, it is easy to understand why she may be fearful of emotions, particularly if in her family history there have been cases where they have caused loss, confusion, addiction and grief.

What part of Teija's chart indicates a fear of achievement and success?
The astrology points to Teija's desire to work on substantial projects with large groups of people involving intensity, confrontation and change (Pluto in the 10th house square Mars in the 8th house). In order to achieve respect and credibility in her career, she is willing to put in long hours of hard work (Mars square Jupiter-Saturn). She has tremendous persistence, stamina and endurance (Saturn-Mars), as well as consistency (Jupiter conjunct Saturn). Indeed the more responsibility

she takes on, the more her career flourishes (Saturn in exaltation). What hinders her is the fact that she will only take action when it feels right (Mars in water) and such hesitancy can at times cause great distress (Mars in the 8th house). She may also find that if her goals are blocked or checked in any way (Mars-Saturn) she is unable to express her anger and frustration and she may instead internalize her feelings, brood about situations and sulk, and become jammed in a sea of emotions which take time to emerge (Mars in water/Mars in fall). This in turn has a knock-on effect, for suppressed anger (Mars-Saturn) can express itself emotionally as depression, or it can express itself physically as a stiffening of the joints, such as arthritis and rheumatism, and a lack of flexibility in both body and mind. There is also the possibility of malignant growths or immune system problems (Mars-Pluto).

What parts of Teija's chart carry inherited issues from her past?

1. The first part comes from her father-figure who carries a deep wound of impotence in some way (myth of the Sun in Leo) expressed through upheaval and change, such as death or financial disaster (Sun in the 8th house/Sun-Mercury trine Neptune).

2. The second part is the fear of taking action, believing it may lead to emotional turmoil (Mars in Cancer in fall). This issue has deep penetration into her family's history (Mars in the 8th house rules both the 4th and 12th houses) suggesting that in the past there have been volatile family agendas (Mars-Pluto) over issues of responsibility (Jupiter-Saturn square Mars) which have ruptured and disrupted the fabric of her family.

What part of Teija's chart suggests she may be fearful of relationships?
Teija has learnt how to relate, socialize and network from her mother and grandmother (Moon-Neptune square Venus), an issue which begins pre-birth when there is a total merging with mother in the womb. This deeply intuitive and boundless bond gets further embedded at birth when, either as the result of a drug-induced birth, a water birth, a music-filled/candlelit birth or a birth where the child is given into the care of her grandmother, there is a blurring for Teija over who is mother and who is child. This lack of physical integrity continues on a body level as susceptibility to allergies and drug sensitivity, and on an emotional level as rapport and compassion or in its more difficult expression as being subject to the emotional whims of others. It impacts on Teija's self-worth (Moon within five degrees of the 2nd house cusp and in the same sign as it) and cascades into her relating pattern as a lack of discrimination in relationships, seeing the world

through rose-coloured glasses and hence seeking Romantic Love (Venus square Neptune). Furthermore, there is a tremendous desire for sensuality and touch in relationships (Venus in Virgo) and at the same time a fear of becoming lost in another person's emotional reality (Moon-Neptune/Venus-Neptune). Hence when young this can express itself as a desire for seclusion (Moon-Neptune). There is, however, the potential for relationships that are different or unusual in some way (Venus in fall), as well as the joy that comes from studying unusual or alternative subjects (Venus in the 9th in fall).

Teija's background

My parents were farmers and I grew up on our farm with them and my grandmother and my little brother. Death in my family irrevocably changed the course of things and I have not continued to be a farmer. Instead learning new things through education and studying seems to be a guideline in my life. My education is Bachelor of Business Administration in the field of library and information services as well as an artisan of decorative and restoration painting. However at the moment I work as a cook in a private home for the elderly and simultaneously learn catering in an adult education center.

My true passion is astrology and I've had the privilege to study this field with Astro Logos. I strongly believe I'm an astrologer in the making! I have studied some psychology and social work in the Open University as well. All I really hope for the future is to find suitable tools for helping and inspiring people and thus creating new ways. Career issues are not easy, I'm hungry for life and many kind of experiences! I have never been in a relationship. I find that a bit weird, but that is just how things have settled. But I think I'm family-orientated too, but it's too soon to ponder these issues. I enjoy life walking to my own drumbeat and take life as it presents itself. I am restless and indeed interested in many, many things in life. I feel as if many options are open at this stage (and age).

What can Teija do to help co-create her 'netivot'?

Teija began a Secondary Progressed New Lunation Phase in August 2000 seeded at 6 degrees Virgo in her 9th house. This twenty-nine and a half years' cycle is concerned with perfecting and polishing her work with finesse and detail in ways that alter and change her philosophy of life, such as through travel, study, teaching, publishing, and so on. In mid-2008 this cycle moves into its First Quarter where the focus is on personal achievement and it stays there until 2012, roughly dovetailing with Teija's Secondary Progressed Moon moving through her 2nd house, with its attention on self-worth, self-esteem and what she values in her life.

Teija completes her first Saturn cycle in 2010 but transiting Saturn conjuncts her natal Saturn only once. In such cases the few years in the lead up to the Saturn Return tend to be more challenging for the person.

Teija's predictive astrology

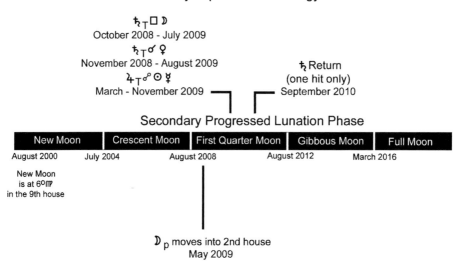

♄ᴛ□ ☽
October 2008 - July 2009

♄ᴛ☌ ♀
November 2008 - August 2009

♄ Return
(one hit only)
September 2010

♃ᴛ☍ ☉ ☿
March - November 2009

Secondary Progressed Lunation Phase

New Moon	Crescent Moon	First Quarter Moon	Gibbous Moon	Full Moon
August 2000	July 2004	August 2008	August 2012	March 2016

New Moon
is at 6°♍
in the 9th house

☽ₚ moves into 2nd house
May 2009

Teija notes that she has 'never been in a relationship'. An overview of the major transits as her Secondary Progressed Moon moves through her 2nd house is as follows:

In 2009 transiting Saturn squares her Moon (loneliness or emotional commitment), and conjuncts her Venus (making or breaking commitments in relationship or restrictions in financial affairs) and transiting Jupiter opposes her Sun-Mercury conjunction (the expansion of her identity and her ideas in the world). If ever Teija was to meet, fall in love with and make a commitment to someone, her predictive work is suggesting that 2009 might be that year.

So how can Teija help her predictive work and coax and coerce it into the shape that she wants? Taking one letter at a time and working with it to fully integrate it before moving on to the next, she can make the following changes:

1. She can begin to slowly move her left hand margin to the right, understanding that her desire for independence does not have to sever the cords from her past but merely release them so they do not continually pull her backwards.

2. She can begin to slowly place the cross bar of her letter 't' at the very top of the stem, recognizing that unless she sets her sights high, she will only ever achieve success below her capabilities.

3. She can become conscious of shaping her letters 'a', 'b', 'g', 'o' and 's' cleanly without any left luggage. As she does so, she may need to delve more deeply into her family's history in order to learn more accurately her family's pattern of emotional disruption, as well as look more deeply at her own emotions and how she can learn to articulate them with clarity.

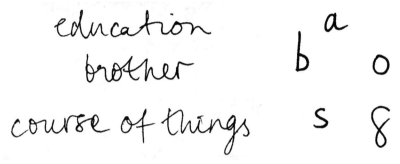

4. She can make sure that her 'i' dots are made cleanly as dots and not jagged hooks.

5. She can begin to make her letter 'f' consistently move through all three landscapes so that it is balanced and therefore encompasses her entire being: body, mind and emotions.

Making alterations to her handwriting one stroke at a time and watching for the small changes that signify shifts in her life, Teija can slowly begin to understand her 'netivot' and work with her handwriting to reshape her life into one that is more fulfilling and satisfying for her. However, along with each handwriting change comes the responsibility to act on what is being offered, for one small change will herald great shifts and many possibilities.

How 'Madison' views enthusiasm

Youth is not a time of life. It's a state of mind. It is a temper of the will, a quality of the imagination, a vigour of the emotions, a predominance of courage over timidity, of the appetite for adventure over the love of ease.

Nobody grows old by merely living a number of years. People grow old only by deserting their ideals. Years wrinkle the skin, but to give up enthusiasm wrinkles the soul.

Whether 60 or 16, there is in every being's heart the love of wonder, the sweet amazement at the stars and starlike things and thoughts, the undaunted challenge of events, the unfailing childlike appetite for what-next, and the joy in the game of living.

You are as young as your faith, as old as your doubt; as young as your self-confidence, as old as your fear; as young as your hope, as old as your despair.

So long as your heart receives messages of beauty, hope, cheer, courage, grandeur and power from the earth, from men and from the Infinite, so long are your young.

Live every day of your life as if you expect to live forever.

Youth is not a time of life. It's a state of mind. It is a temper of the will, a quality of the imagination, a vigour of the emotions, a predominance of courage over timidity, of the appetite for adventure over the love of ease.

Madison has written this piece in black ink on an unlined white matt silk paper. She begins writing close to the top of the page, indicating familiarity with the recipient, and sustains balanced margins all around, showing a balanced relationship with her past and her future. As well, her handwriting shows even spacing between each word and between each line, suggesting clarity of thought and organizational ability. However, in order to sustain consistency of line spacing, Madison has had to write through the swollen valley loops of her letters 'g' 'j', 'q' and 'y'. Thus they appear to crash into the mountain landscapes of her next line of writing. This suggests an ability to arrange her practical world but an inability to plan too far ahead, possibly due to the abundance of unconscious emotions and instincts which become entangled with and flood her mind, her imagination and her intellect and blurs what inspires her and creates her goals.

The base of Madison's writing alters as she moves down the page. It begins level in the first few paragraphs (initially goal-orientated, disciplined and focused on her plans), then falls at the end of the second paragraph (feels over-worked and discouraged). It then changes to rising lines by the fourth paragraph (optimistic, creative and enthusiastic once again) and completes as convex lines in the final paragraph (enthusiasm tails off due to lack of energy).

Her letters are written with a vertical slant, suggesting that she does not readily show her emotions. Instead she tends to be independent and appears self-assured, is calm in times of stress and works well under pressure. It is also simplified writing: letters that would normally carry loops into the mountain region ('b', 'd', 'f', 'h', 'k', 'l', 't') are written with a straight stroke, showing a desire to reach her goals with the least possible hindrance. This gives her a quick grasp of situations and an ability to understand the essence of a subject but it denies her the fully-formed loop that contains her inspiration, her imagination and her unique creativity. As well, Madison writes with a heavy pressure, suggesting physical energy, willpower and a love of strong colours. However, it can also indicate a heaviness of spirit caused by inner tension and suppressed energy. This trait of heavy pressure combined with writing that runs through her valley loops suggests that, whilst Madison can frame the bigger picture of her life, there may be so many events occurring in her life that her ability to prioritize has disappeared.

Madison connects most of her letters within each word, suggesting she has a sense of purpose, good mental co-ordination and is a logical thinker, as well as someone who forms friendships easily and can maintain a flow of conversation.

Her handwriting is angular, indicating that she seeks challenges, is persistent, and has an intellectual approach to her practical world. It also suggests she is a hard worker, self-disciplined, possesses strong will-power and can work alone with ease, and that she readily takes on responsibility. However, it can also suggest someone who is somewhat rigid in their approach, with little flexibility or tolerance. This can, over time, create anxiety as well as accumulate unexpressed anger. Angular writing also belongs to people who are critically-minded, who use logic rather than emotions in their approach to their work. In its best expression this is someone with analytical strength; in its more difficult expression this can be someone who is judgemental of others.

Madison writes her capital 'I' as a single stroke, suggesting she wishes to be seen for who she is. Her 'i' dots are written as points and in most cases sit directly above the 'i' stem, some quite high, suggesting accuracy and precision in thinking. She crosses her letter 't' from left to right relatively high up the stem and within her mountain landscape, giving her an evenhanded outlook and setting high goals for herself. However, she writes her letter 'f' as a fishhook with a flick to the right of the letter as it completes in her valley landscape, a trait that is repeated in her letter 'y' ('quality', 'timidity', nobody', years') also in her valley landscape, as well as in her letter 't' ('it', 'to', 'Whether', 'heart', 'sweet') in the plains landscape. These flicks or ticks suggest unconscious aggression, some emerging from her emotions and others connected with her practical world. The piece of art that is created by these shapes is of someone who has been told off or 'ticked off' when little and whose voice has now become part of Madison's subconscious self-talk as she attempts to move forward (right movement) in her life. Sometimes Madison adds a hook to the left part of the cross-bar of her letter 't' ('time', 'the', appetite'), indicating something in her practical world that is hooking her back into the past.

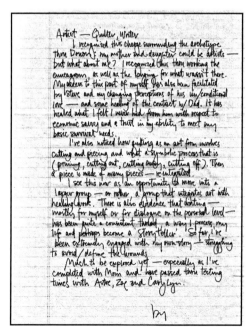

Madison's spontaneous writing

Madison's spontaneous writing is written on lined yellow notepad paper and whilst she does not write on the lines, she does adhere to the line spacing and hugs the printed left hand margin. This suggests that, although Madison demands the right to express her originality (writing above the lines), using someone else's frameworks allows her to stay focused on her goals and plans. Without such guides, Madison's attention wanders and her energy is rapidly depleted.

How Madison's chart speaks to her through her handwriting

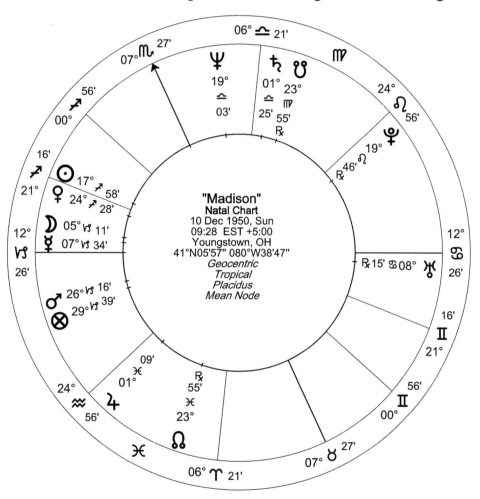

What parts of Madison's chart contain unconscious anxiety and rigidity?

1. People see Madison as responsible (Capricorn Ascendant) and able to solve problems (ruler of the Ascendant is Saturn as the apex planet of the T-Square with the Moon-Mercury and Uranus). However, such responsibility may have been placed upon her shoulders at a relatively young age as the result of issues in her parents' relationship (Mercury conjunct the Moon in opposition to Uranus lies across the relating axis), possibly involving business matters (Mercury) which may have undergone upheaval and change (Mercury rules Virgo which is intercepted in the 8th house/Saturn is in the 8th house). As such, without the experience of maturity, Madison may have continually felt that she did not know enough and in order to counter this, may have become a workaholic with an underlying inferiority complex. Furthermore, whilst Madison actively seeks challenges (cardinal T-Square), this configuration asks her to input continual effort that never seems to relax its grip (Saturn in exaltation) and as such, never allows her to fully appreciate her ability to shape (Saturn-Mercury/Mercury in Capricorn) her unusual thinking (Mercury-Uranus).

2. People also see Madison as someone whose feelings influence her thinking (Moon conjunct Mercury in Capricorn conjunct the Ascendant). This pattern began at birth where some form of drama or upheaval (Saturn in the 8th) possibly involving technological intervention (Moon-Uranus) meant that Madison was taken away from her mother for a short time, resulting in separation anxiety (Moon in Capricorn/Moon-Saturn). As a neo-natal deprived of physical contact with her mother, her smell, the sound of her heartbeat and nourishment from her body, Madison's emotional distress overwhelmed her perceptions (Moon-Mercury), leading to a distrust of her body and her feelings (Moon-Uranus). Embedded was the struggle between insight and clarity of thinking (Mercury-Uranus) and rapidly learning to use her intellect to solve emotional issues (Moon-Uranus) versus painful emotions which overwhelm and cloud her thinking (Moon-Mercury). One way Madison learns to handle such pain is to suppress and dominate what appear to her to be irrational emotions (Saturn as the ruler of the Ascendant, the dispositor of the Moon-Mercury in Capricorn and the apex of the T-Square and exalted). This need to control has the option to ease once she forms a caring, committed relationship (the Moon rules the 7th house) where she can process her feelings within a safe structure. She can also help this aspect by learning from people who value painful emotions (Moon-Saturn/Saturn rules the 2nd house and Uranus has affinity with the 2nd house) how to think whilst feeling (Moon-Mercury).

3. The third area of Madison's chart concerns hidden family agendas many generations old regarding issues of trust and betrayal (Sun close to the cusp of the 12th house and in the same sign as it, ruling the 8th house, and square to the nodal axis), deception and disillusion (Sun sextile Neptune) by the men of her tribe. This issue was imprinted from her father-figure whom Madison sees as carrying a long-suffering physical or emotional wound. The myth of the Sun in Sagittarius is that of Chiron, the centaur, who is wounded in the thigh by a poisoned arrow but being immortal cannot die, so it is a festering wound which is only healed when Chiron changes places with Prometheus, representing the gift of intellect. She also sees him as lost, weakened or absent (Sun close to the cusp of the 12th house/Sun sextile Neptune/Sun trine Pluto) and in his absence becomes idealized (Venus sextile Neptune). This behaviour then cascades into every relationship she forms thereafter until she can learn to change the pattern. With no model from her father-figure for how to initiate and take action in the world, she learns to approach the world with an innocence often termed naivety or gullibility (Venus sextile Neptune). The price she pays for this is a lack of integrity and blurred boundaries with others. Until she learns, slowly and painfully, how to develop her own inner wisdom, relying on a feminine or yin model of self-trust (Sun-Pluto), the path of her grandmother or the women in her tribe (Sun-Neptune), either in the field of the arts or healing or spirituality, then she will continually be faced with issues of disillusion and betrayal.

What part of Madison's chart indicates areas of weakness and depletion?

Madison is motivated by touch, sensuality, practicality, structure and results (Mars in Capricorn). However, she may also have found that her energy can be easily drained by other people (Mars square Neptune) and that she may begin projects with verve and then find her enthusiasm waning. Such actions may manifest as a lack of focus and feeling exhausted, particularly in terms of academic learning or travel (Neptune in the 9th) which she may not value until she is older (Neptune has an affinity with Pisces intercepted in the 2nd house). This aspect, also known as the 'Clark Kent-Superman syndrome', works best when spiritual, artistic or metaphysical energy can be harnessed through the muscles with practices such as yoga or T'ai Chi, ballroom dancing, or even power-walking. By turning inwards to utilize this energy, Madison finds that her drive and motivation increases.

Madison's background

I grew up in rural Pennsylvania in the mix of incredible earth beauty and economic deprivation. My parents split just as I finished high school, and I moved to southern California in 1968 with my mother. I spent the next decade working in restaurants, doing drugs, getting a degree and generally wandering off course toward any taboo I could wrestle. At nineteen I'd had a daughter who I gave up for adoption. At twenty-eight, I chose a homebirth for my bi-racial daughter, Astre. Two years later, at my Saturn Return, I moved to England with my daughter and married a New Zealander. We returned to northern California in 1986. Over the next twenty years I raised three wonderful children while building a newsletter business with my journalist husband and producing extensive textile art. We had many opportunities for travel around the US and internationally. I've also been actively involved with a healing paradigm called 'Integrated Awareness' for over fifteen years. I also made contact with my grown daughter who was adopted, and we've had an evolving relationship during those years, including grandchildren.

During the past five years, as I thought the pressures would ease as my children got older, instead I was primary in assisting my mother through her final years. As my youngest daughter left home for college, I realized the next big shift needed to happen with my marriage. We've separated and recognized we've completed what we agreed to do together and are settling our process equitably and with love. So at last, I have my own independent pathway. I'm studying for my international certification in astrology and in late 2009 I begin an MA course in Cultural Astronomy and Astrology (University of Wales, Lampeter, UK). I dream of bringing the wealth of skills I have cultivated over my life to a new level of expression – in seeing clients, perhaps researching and writing, certainly travelling. I dream of looking at the night sky and seeing the constellated stories there.

As I have allowed myself to dream and take bigger risks and ask for more for myself, more of my dreams come true! I am currently moving to live at a rural retreat centre among the rolling hills where the starry sky is so visible. I am living there with a new partner who meets me both emotionally and spiritually. I feel this joyfulness that is an awakening of my core self: I am actively moving toward what is my life purpose in this phase of my life. I feel so alive!

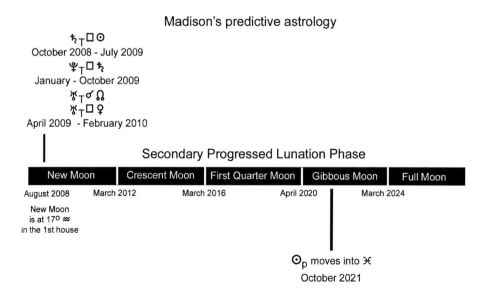

144

What can Madison do to help co-create her 'netivot'?

Madison began a Secondary Progressed New Lunation Phase in August 2008 at 17 degrees Aquarius in her 1st house. This twenty-nine and a half years' cycle will focus on how she develops her unique ideas and concepts within new groups and how she is able to help those groups as a result. As if underlining this, in 2009 Madison encounters a whole new group of people who shift her life path (transiting Uranus conjunct the North Node) and change her social networks (transiting Uranus square Venus), at the same time pushing her to take on new responsibilities (transiting Saturn square the Sun) through projects that require her to work extremely hard (transiting Pluto square Saturn).

In 2021 when Madison is seventy-one years of age and in her Secondary Progressed Gibbous lunation phase, her Secondary Progressed Sun moves into Pisces. Whilst this is a long way ahead, Madison has dreams she wants to bring to fruition and she is still planting seeds. Therefore she can encourage the form of those dreams through the handwriting changes she makes now.

So how can Madison help her predictive work and coax and coerce it into the shape that she wants? Taking one letter at a time and working with it to fully integrate it before moving on to the next, she can make the following changes:

1. She can slowly begin to lessen the swollen loops of her letters 'g', 'j', 'q' and 'y' in her valley landscape, taking care not to write through the loops on each successive line. Hauling back the loops in this way then becomes a stimulus for Madison every time she writes to think whilst feeling and so learn to prioritize what she wants to accomplish.

2. She can change her letter 't' cross-stroke and stem by lifting her pen off the paper to avoid a flick or a hook and begin to release old 'self-talk', and at the same time slowly raise the 't' cross-bar to the top of the stem so that her exalted Saturn can reach as high as she wants to achieve.

3. She can change her letter 'f', and her letter 'y' when it ends a word, to avoid the right flick in her valley landscape.

4. Given that her Secondary Progressed Sun will eventually move into Pisces, she can slowly change her letter 'g' to a 'figure of eight' 'g' to allow her creative essence to pour more effectively from her.

5. She can relax the grip on her pen so that there is not so much pressure applied to page, thus releasing the pressure under which she puts herself.

6. She can lift her pen off the page as she makes her letter 's' and so avoid embedding it with left luggage.

7. She can soften her letter 'e' to make sure it does not contain angles, or change it to a Greek 'e' to allow her creativity to flow.

As her new Secondary Progressed Lunation cycle begins, this is an ideal time for Madison to create her 'wish list' for the next twenty-nine and a half years. More importantly, working with her predictive work and focusing on making slow changes to her handwriting, she can help to shape her path so that she strengthens what has previously been weak and builds on strengths she has already fashioned from previous Seconday Progressed Lunation cycles. As she does this, so her 'netivot' becomes clear for her and so she treads those paths with more certainty and greater fulfilment.

How 'Mallory' views enthusiasm

Youth is not a time of life. It's a state of mind. It is a temper of will, a quality of the imagination, a vigour of the emotions, a predominance of courage over a timidity, of the appetite for adventure over love of ease.

Nobody grows old by merely living a number of years. People grow old only by deserting their ideals. Years wrinkle the skin, but to give up enthusiasm wrinkles the soul.

Whether 60 or 16, there is in every being's heart the love of wonder, the sweet amazement at the stars and starlike things and thoughts, the undaunted challenge of events, the unfailing childlike appetite for what-next, and the joy in the game of living

You are as young as your faith, as old as your doubt; as young as your self-confidence, as old as your fears; as young as your hope, as old as your despair.

So long as your heart receives messages of beauty, hope, cheer, courage, grandeur and power from the earth, from men and from the infinite, so long are you young.

Live every day of your life as if you expected to live forever.

Youth is not a time of life. It's a state of mind. It is a temper of will, a quality of the imagination, a vigour of the emotions, a predominance of courage over a timidity, of the appetite for adventure over love of ease.

Mallory writes on white unlined paper in royal blue ink. This piece is written with a relatively narrow, straight margin on the left hand side, indicating someone who has a healthy regard for the past and who is self-disciplined. She maintains balanced word spacing and line spacing, with no mingling of letters, suggesting that on the broad level of life she displays an ability to organize her time and effort, to think constructively and with a sense of direction.

However, her handwriting contains a mix of slants, some letters written vertically, some towards the left, and some towards the right, reflecting someone who is pulled in all directions, with a lack of self-discipline and strong inner contradictions. This is an indication of immaturity, despite a person's age. It suggests that an incident occurred around puberty which undermined her self-esteem and frustrated her ambitions, and produced compulsively frozen behaviour from that time onwards and which is now emerging through the handwriting as a cry for help.

Underlining this low self-esteem, Mallory's handwriting also contains a mix of directions, rising upwards at the beginning of the piece and slanting downwards by the second to last paragraph, suggesting that she begins an enterprise with optimism and commitment which, towards the end, turns to anxiety, fatigue, and pessimism.

As well, Mallory's letter shapes are highly irregular, for example, her letter 't' is written with the cross-bar crossed at the top of the stem for 'Youth' (high ambitions), well below the top sitting in the practical plains landscape for 'not' (lowering her ambitions to ones she feels she can achieve), crossed only on the left and quite high up the stem for 'time' (begins projects well but can't finish them), with a stem written as a loop in 'It's' (hidden concerns connected with ambition), and with the cross-bar covering the next letter in 'temper' (self-assured with strong opinions). Such a span of options implies a struggle between confidence and doubt.

The mountain sweeps of Mallory's letters 'h' ('the'), 'k' ('wrinkle') and 'l' ('people', 'living') either contain angles or flames, suggesting that she intellectualizes what inspires her, or else they are written with square tops ('will', 'only', 'their', 'soul') signifying conscious or unconscious tendencies towards aggression. This latter issue of unconscious hostility is reinforced in the leftward flicks of the valley loops of her letter 'y' ('by', 'you', 'young') symptomatic of an issue from the past. This is reinforced by the self-talk in the angular top of Mallory's letter 'e' ('emotions', 'over', 'deserting', 'events'), an internal voice repeating 'that would never work'. Mallory sets up obstacles for herself before she has even begun.

Mallory's handwriting also contains angles in the valley landscapes of her letters 'g' and 'y' ('living', 'young') showing that she uses her intellect to solve emotional issues. In so doing, she robs herself of the awe of life and the ability to look at the familiar with new eyes.

As well, when Mallory writes her letters 'a', 'c', 'd' and 'g', the initial movement of the letter covers itself, giving rise to a double action. Since the double-stressed parts of these letters occur in her plains landscape, they represent anxiety resulting in severe inhibitions and self-protection, the need to conceal something extremely deep and personal from other people. This is emphasized in her letter 'c' ('challenge', 'childlike', 'cheer') which contains an initial resentment hook. There are also hooks at the end of some of her letter 't' cross-bars.

The plump loops of some of her letter 'd' stems contain sensitivity and unreleased emotions. They are found in the handwriting of people who take the burdens of others onto their shoulders and then suffer in silence, lack the confidence to ask for what they truly want, and often end up blaming others. This may then account for the tiny constricted loop on her letter 'g' which indicates emotional suppression, suggesting that Mallory's energy is channeled into more absorbing practical work. This is emphasized in such words as 'predominance', 'imagination', 'timidity' where all letters are joined together, suggesting someone who is constricted by logic and predictability. In writing such words there is no lifting of the pen to ease the constriction. Mallory does not pause to take a breath. Instead she pushes on to the bitter end, putting up with the mental strain of working under pressure. This is emphasized by 'i' dots and 't' bars which, from time to time, are omitted ('faith', 'earth',' unfailing', 'despair') indicating someone who is anxious to get to the goal by the quickest route possible.

Over all Mallory's handwriting could be described as square with angles, representative of a highly conventional person who would rather take the line of least resistance than confront, who rejects her intuition, keeping a closed mind to anything new or not already understood whilst being plagued by inner conflict.

Mallory's spontaneous handwriting

This piece is written in purple ink on a cream coloured paper. It shows the same attributes as the previous piece with the following added information: in her spontaneous writing Mallory hugs the left hand side of the page leaving no margin, suggesting someone who is dominated by her past. She writes her personal pronoun 'I' with serifs, indicating confidence. However, the serifs mostly slope downwards, suggesting a pessimistic outlook. She writes her 'th' as a ligature, indicating a fluid creative thinker, yet there are no 'i' dots whatsoever, indicating forgetfulness and lack of concentration.

How Mallory's chart speaks to her through her handwriting

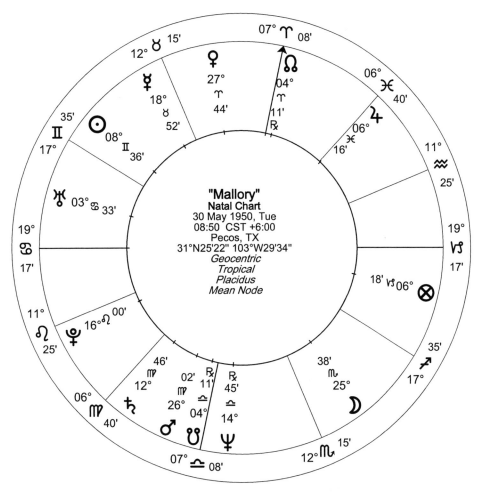

"Mallory"
Natal Chart
30 May 1950, Tue
08:50 CST +6:00
Pecos, TX
31°N25'22" 103°W29'34"
Geocentric
Tropical
Placidus
Mean Node

What part of Mallory's chart reveals anxiety and suggests there may be a battle between intellect and emotion?

People see Mallory as emotionally nurturing and at times emotionally needy (Cancer Ascendant), as well as a person whose emotional security is derived from being able to solve problems (ruler of the Ascendant is the Moon as part of the Moon-Mercury-Pluto T-Square). However, embedded into this aspect is a birth scenario of trauma and intensity (Moon in Scorpio/Moon-Pluto), resulting in Mallory forming an intense, deeply-emotional, non-superficial bond with her mother – a survival mechanism which is inextricably mixed with anxiety and obsession (Mercury-Pluto). Hence Mallory's thinking is continually flooded with worries and concerns ignited by her mother and all things emotional (Moon-

Mercury/Mercury rules the 12th house). This interior climate deeply impacts on her self-esteem and personal resources (apex planet of the T-Square is in the 2nd house).

What parts of Mallory's chart affect her confidence?

1. Mallory has inherited a problem-solving pattern from her father-figure (Sun in 11th as apex planet of Saturn-Jupiter-Sun T-Square), that of utilizing steadfastness and methodical consistency (Jupiter-Saturn) in the area of education and study (3rd-9th axis) to achieve success in groups (Sun in 11th). So Mallory will readily take on responsibility when young and work extremely hard in order to gain her father-figure's approval and fulfill his expectations of her (Sun-Saturn). However, this is a three-tiered family pattern, involving her larger-than-life, risk-taking, successful paternal grandfather (Sun-Jupiter/Jupiter in rulership in Pisces trine Uranus). This pattern has been paradoxically transmitted to his son (Mallory's father) as caution, control and fear of failure (Sun square Saturn), fear of being undermined (Sun trine Neptune/Neptune conjunct the IC in the 4th house) and fear of being different (Uranus in the 12th house), and passed on to Mallory. This in turn affects her self-esteem and translates into an inability to complete projects and a tendency to self-sabotage due to fear of failure. By never finishing projects, she never has to achieve her goals and handle success.

2. This is reinforced by another inherited family pattern (unaspected Venus/ Venus as dispositor of the South Node), a two-layered one in which Mallory sees social networks as a challenge (Venus in Aries), particularly in connection with her career (Venus in the 10th house), rushing headlong into relationships and then feeling anger and regret when such actions cause upheaval; or else feels as if she has no ability at all to be socially interactive (the on-again/off-again quality of an unaspected planet).

Mallory's background

My mother was an orphan in a Northern Arizona community of Mormons. She was four when her mother died. When she was six years old, her relatives decided that a young girl should not stay on a ranch with her father and two brothers. They moved her into a succession of relatives' households where she did housework and childcare. My father was brought up in an Irish-Catholic household in Texas. He had seven brothers and one sister. All of the brothers pooled their resources to successively put each other through college. The Depression showed my dad the unreliability of employed work, so he began a company, which was at first shipping and later, became a fertilizer manufacturing company. He invited his brothers to join him, which all but one did.

I was a caesarean birth as my mother had a hip structure that was too narrow. She reported that I was born with my head looking misshapen. In childhood I was hearing impaired due to chronic fluid in the ears. This was discovered and repaired when I was five. My walking was delayed due to ear/balance problems and my speech was unintelligible due to the former hearing impairment. In school, I would try to hide behind children to avoid having to speak in class. I was picked on. My mother would hide me from her visiting friends due to feeling shame for having a retarded or handicapped child. I spent a year in speech therapy. I felt I must hide my true and shameful self and pretend to be 'normal'. I could not let people know how fearful and lost I felt for then they might permanently send me to the handicapped school and then I would lose all face with my family, and their love, if that were to happen. My sister was belittling to me at home, and I had no friends at school.

We moved every two to three years because of my father's work. This made it difficult to catch up in elementary studies. I was on the outside of most social circles until I was a teenager. My father was my best friend as a child. I was his sidekick. He was my best friend, but he also had a terrible temper that sometimes made him a potentially terrifying figure.

My sister became pregnant, left home, and married quite early. This made my life at home easier as my sister was unfriendly, however I did miss her presence. I was teased at school due to her being a 'bad girl'. We moved due to the reputation given from her situation. We moved to a place where I finally found a social life.

I developed a group of friends in high school that I enjoyed. Later, when I went to college in Northern California, I studied music and theatre. Following college, I moved to San Francisco with a boyfriend whom I later married. (February 1972). This was a disaster. We divorced in 1975 and due to an invitation by my parents, I moved to Phoenix Arizona and studied Speech Pathology in 1976. I was able to maintain a 3.8 GPA there, but ran into difficulty with what I perceived to be sexual harassment. By the time I was near graduating with my Master's in late 1980, I was so stressed out that I was having difficulties with remembering what I studied. One of the harassing instructors bragged to me that he would 'burn me out'. The sexual pressure continued, and I began to doubt my ability as my grades fell. I am still not sure that I am not learning disabled in some way. Because I could be employed without the Master's degree, I did not go back to complete it. I was afraid to go back.

I received a call on December 12,1982, that my father had crashed his airplane into a hillside. My mother and I knew it was suicide, as he had hinted about doing exactly this. He had begun a mining venture in Costa Rica after his brother took over their company. The mafia/government of Costa Rica tried to extort money from him and threatened his life with thugs and machine guns. When it looked as if he might fail there, and lose face with his brothers, he crashed his airplane in Benson, Arizona. My mother was distraught, so I moved to Green Valley to live with her for a year.

Following that, I moved to Tucson and worked for a private speech clinic. I bought a house. I had a good relationship with a life partner between 1989 and 1999. His diabetic condition began to cause blindness and later put him on home dialysis. On 9-9-99, the day before his diabetes appointment to get a kidney transplant, he committed suicide by structuring a blood sugar hypoglycaemic attack.

It took me awhile to recover from this. After a year of recovery, I was able to get back a few of my long-standing Speech Pathology clients, whom I still see when I go into Tucson. I also go into Tucson to maintain my old home. Currently, I live with my mother in Sahuarita, Arizona. She uses a walker and needs someone here to make sure she does not fall. I would love to hire more home care for her, but it is too expensive, and my devotion to the Persephone myth requires me spend part of my time with her (just joking, I think).

My Saturn return occurs in September, 2008. Already, I feel my life imploding. There are two-fold stresses: my duties to my sick mother (since 2005 and increasing in severity) which have made me feel a prisoner. I will be there full time and will have to hire help if I am to keep my house in Tucson, much less any of my friends. The second stress is a knowledge that what has become apparent to me in my study of astrology, is likely a Saturn theme in my life: I skip past the drill and discipline required for elementary study in an area and jump to the conclusions and graduate level. Later, I wonder why my foundations in that area are weak and my long term memory in the area is superficial. This is a crisis point for me, in that it has likely been a major disrupting point in all of my goals up to this point in my life. I feel I must start over, once again. I am grateful for receiving this understanding, albeit so late in life. I want to prepare for the future. I need help with this upcoming return of Saturn to my natal position.

Mallory's predictive astrology

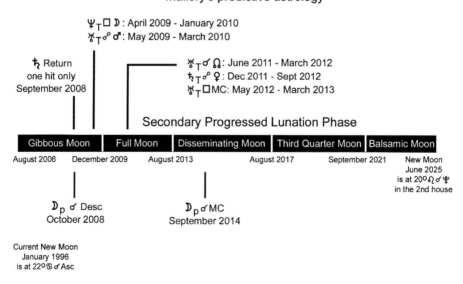

What can Mallory do to help co-create her 'netivot'?

How can Mallory help shape her predictive work so that she feels less like a prisoner in caring for her mother? How can she learn to set solid foundations and take care of the details for the goals she wants to accomplish? In January 1996 Mallory began a Secondary Progressed Lunation cycle seeded at 22 degrees Cancer conjunct her Ascendant. This cycle is concerned with having a far more independent and creative role in her world. In 2014 Mallory's Secondary Progressed Moon conjuncts her MC, offering her public success or change of status. How can Mallory capitalize on this potentially fruitful time in her life?

Given Mallory's history and the fact that she is now living with her mother in order to care for her, the obvious natal issue that requires nourishment is her relationship with her mother (Moon-Mercury-Pluto T-Square), along with her fear of failure (Jupiter-Saturn-Sun T-Square).

Mallory has been concerned about her upcoming second Saturn Return. However, transiting Saturn only makes one pass to its natal placement (in September 2008). Instead, beginning in October 2008, Mallory is being asked to re-evaluate her commitments (Secondary Progressed Moon conjunct her Descendant) and, in 2009, handle the issues around caring for her mother (transiting Neptune square her Moon) along with a great deal of anger or passion (transiting Uranus opposition Mars). In 2012 there are sudden changes to her social status (transiting Uranus conjuncts the MC) and either the making or breaking of commitments in relationships and/or a restriction upon her financial affairs (transiting Saturn opposition Venus).

Knowing that Mallory has until 2014 to reset the course of her life allows her to slowly look at her natal issues. To help her transits express themselves in the most fruitful way, and taking one letter at a time and consciously altering its shape in conjunction with her predictive work, Mallory can make the following changes:

1. She can maintain consistency with the slant of her letters, writing them vertically or towards the right, to focus her direction and self-discipline.

2. She can maintain consistency with her line direction. In this case it may be useful for Mallory to write on lined paper for a month as she brings new structures into her thinking, planning and goal-setting.

3. She can reshape her letters 'a', 'c', 'd' and 'g', eliminating the initial covering movement as well as any hooks in her letter 'c' and at end of her letter 't' cross-bars.

courage quality a

undaunted d d

4. She can begin to make her personal pronoun 'I' serifs consistent so that they support her sense of self.

Ɪ I

5. She can lift her pen off the page, putting spaces between the letters of long words to give space for her intuition.

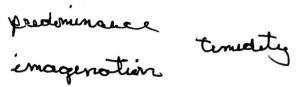

6. She can begin to reshape her letter 't' to eliminate unwanted luggage and slowly place the cross bar at the very top of the stem, drawn evenly from left to right and angled slightly upward to help her set and achieve her goals, recognizing that unless she sets her sights high, she will only ever achieve success below her capabilities.

7. She can work at softening the angles that appear in the mountain loops of her letters 'h', 'k', and 'l'.

8. She can work at eliminating the leftward flicks of the valley loops of her letters 'y' and 'g' and the angular top of her letter 'e' (see 'wrinkle' above).

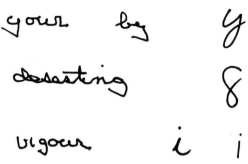

9. She can work at making clear 'i' dots placed directly above the 'i' stem.

10. She can reshape her 'd' stem so that it is clear of withheld emotions.

All of the above changes represent changes to deep-seated emotional difficulties that have been protecting Mallory for many years, so she needs to approach them with care and gentleness. By making alterations to her handwriting one shape at a time in conjunction with her predictive work, and watching for the small changes in her life that signify shifts of attitude and reveal her 'netivot', Mallory can begin to approach her goals with greater confidence. As she reshapes her handwriting, so Mallory can start to reshape her life into one that is more pleasing and less frustrating for her, understanding that one small change has the potential to change her life dramatically.

How 'Olivia' views enthusiasm

Youth is not a time of life. It's a state of mind. It's a temper of the will, a quality of the imagination, a vigour of the emotions, a predominance of courage over timidity, of the appetite for adventure over love of ease.

Nobody grows old by merely living a number of years. People grow old by deserting their ideals. Years wrinkle the skin, but to give up enthusiasm wrinkles the soul.

Whether 16 or 60, there is in every being's heart the love of wonder, the sweet amazement at the stars and starlike things and thoughts, the undaunted challenge of events, the unfailing childlike appetite for what-next, and the joy in the game of living.

You are as young as your faith, as old as you doubt, as young as your self-confidence as old as your fear, as young as your hope, as old as your despair.

So long as your heart receives messages of beauty, hope, cheer, courage, grandeur and power from the earth, from men and from the Infinite, so long are you young.

Live every day of your life as if you expect to live forever.

Youth is not a time of life. It's a state of mind. It's a temper of the will, a quality of the imagination, a vigour of the emotions, a predominance of courage over timidity, of the appetite for adventure over love of ease.

Olivia writes on lined paper using a fountain pen. In choosing to write with a fountain pen, Olivia makes a statement about how she wants to be seen by the world. Writing with a fountain pen forces a person to slow their writing down for legibility, hence it allows Olivia to express her fine taste and sensuality.

The slant of her handwriting is upright, indicating that she thinks before she acts placing intellect ahead of impulse, and the predominant focus of her letters lie in her plains landscape, suggesting that the practical world of everyday occurrences takes most of her attention.

Her handwriting hugs both the left hand vertical guide line and the hortizontal lines, signifying that she prefers others to set the rules. At the same time she writes to the edge of the right hand page, indicating that she will make decisions rapidly but can lack tact and be seen as over-enthusiastic. Indeed the extended final stroke of her captial 'N' indicates intiative and enterprise, and a willing enthusiasm to explore new ideas. Her handwriting is even and incorporates a balanced distance between words, and she is careful not to crash the lower loops in her valley landscape of one line into the mountain sweeps of the next, both traits expressing a fine awareness of the space between herself and others, as well as clarity of thought and organizing ability. Overall this is the handwriting of someone who creates steadiness and structure inside another's framework.

However, as one looks deeper into the detail, Olivia's handwriting tells two quite different stories within several single patterns:

1. The loops of Olivia's valley landscape letters are either rounded and full, indicating a strong, active imagination, along with creative or artistic tendencies, or else rounded, open and wide which shows a warm nature with a degree of emotional immaturity and/or naiviety.

2. Olivia's letters are connected to each other through undulating, friendly writing, indicating the willingness for co-operation with others and a desire to share experiences and thoughts. Yet in contrast the shape of most of the letters are square, suggestive of a closed mind, of someone who consciously or unconsciously rejects their instinctual drives and thus may be seen as narrow-minded.

3. Her letter 't' cross-bar vacillates between being drawn across the top and linked with the following letter when she writes 'th', indicating a fluid thinker with soaring ambitions or else is written low on the stem and to the right of it ('not', 'state', 'adventure') indicating that she finishes projects well but is not willing to stretch herself in order to do so. Sometimes the bar extends over other following letters ('appetite', 'timidity', 'adventure') suggesting over-caring behaviour, and at other times it is detached from the stem ('timidity', 'thoughts') suggesting unrealistic ideals.

4. The two capital 'Y' letters are written quite differently. 'Years wrinkle the soul' is written as a 'V' cone and then completed with a sharp angle which stabs into her valley landscape, suggesting unconscious aggression around her emotions. 'Youth' and 'You' are written as a 'U' and then completed with a rounded but closed bowl in her plains landscape, suggesting plans which slosh around in a basin and go nowhere.

5. Her letter 'f' is mostly written as a stick in her mountain landscape but with a full belly protruding into her valley landscape. This is the letter 'f' written by someone who is either relying on someone else to shape their ideas or who is continually manifesting someone else's plans.

6. Her letter 'o' is written with a container on its right hand side, indicating that Olivia is keeping secret issues or confidences for others. This is mirrored in her letter 'b'. In some cases she completely encircles her letter 'o' ('vigour', 'courage', 'old') and her letter 'a' ('a', 'imagination', 'predominance') suggesting the secrets she is keeping are slowly strangling her.

7. Finally, on letters that would normally include sweeps up into the mountains – 'f', 'h', 'k', 'l' – there are none, suggesting that Olivia has either deliberately powered down the challenges she sets for herself, and exchanged the role of her imagination and inspiration for a more grounded and practical reality, or that the attrition of life has worn this from her.

Taken as a whole her handwriting indicates that she is caught in a double-bind: the desire to achieve something for herself but enslaved to other people's plans. This may be the handwriting of someone who feels that the only way she can express her sensitive and imaginative side is via the pen with which she writes.

How Olivia's chart speaks to her through her handwriting

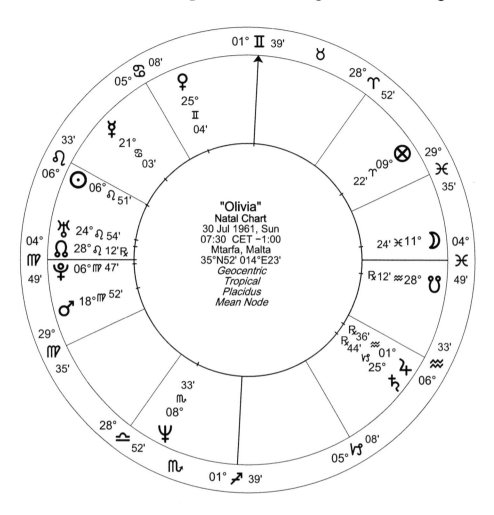

"Olivia"
Natal Chart
30 Jul 1961, Sun
07:30 CET −1:00
Mtarfa, Malta
35°N52' 014°E23'
Geocentric
Tropical
Placidus
Mean Node

What parts of Olivia's chart describe her vacillation between assertion and submission?

1. The first part describes how Olivia is seen by the world. Olivia is seen as someone who conveys intensity, persistence and quiet strength (Pluto conjunct the Asc) built upon communication skills (Scorpio intercepted in the 3rd house). This is interwoven with a profound emotional empathy for others, intially embodied for her by her mother (Moon opposition Pluto/Moon in Pisces). On the one hand Olivia experiences her mother as powerful and intensely emotional (Moon-Pluto) which

can be overwhelming for her (Moon in Pisces in the 7th house); on the other, it is through her mother that she learns to gain emotional fulfillment (Moon in the 7th house). Through this double-bind model of relationship Olivia is drawn into the same emotional power struggles in committed relationships, both business and personal, and may find she must continually assert her independence.

2. The second part describes what drives Olivia and how she takes action. Olivia is motivated by her own learning, ideas, analysis and detail (Mars in Virgo in the 1st house drawing in the 3rd-9th axis of education by rulership and interception) which she shares with her partner (Mars opposition Moon in the 7th). Nevertheless, in so doing, she may find herself caught in an empathic, emotional grip (Mars in opposition to the Moon) which turns into a power struggle (Moon-Pluto)

3. The third part concerns the manner in which Olivia relates to others. Olivia is skilled at social networking (Venus in the 10th house square Mars in the 1st house) formed through her education and learning (Venus also drawing in the 3rd-9th axis of education by rulership and interception). From this she gains opportunities to be socially gregarious (Venus sextile Uranus conjunct the North Node in the 12th house), yet in so doing she will encounter her family's fear of being different (Uranus in the 12th house).

What part of Olivia's chart indicates that she is happy to work within other people's frameworks to create steadiness and structure?
Behind the intensity of Pluto on her Ascendant Olivia is seen as an empathic communicator (ruler of the Ascendant is Mercury in Cancer) whose insights come when she is emotionally receptive to others (Mercury in Cancer). In its best expression she can take those insights and shape them into constructive information (Mercury opposition Saturn/Saturn in rulership) in groups (Mercury in the 11th house) by means of her creativity (5th-11th axis); or using the insights she gains from working with groups, she can feed them back into her own creative work (5th-11th axis/Saturn in the 5th house). However, unless Olivia is willing to take on the responsibility and hard work required to achieve creative fulfillment for herself (Saturn in rulership in the 5th house and ruling the 6th house), she may find herself trapped by needy people who require her time and attention to solve their problems. This may be her own children, or people with whom she socializes (5th-11th axis).

What patterns in Olivia's chart contain family issues that have the potential to stifle her?

1. The first is a pattern that has been inherited through her father and her paternal grandparents (cadent T-Square: Sun in Leo in the 12th house opposition Jupiter in Aquarius within 5 degrees of the 6th house cusp square Neptune as the apex planet in the 3rd house) and describes the lost, weakened or absent men in her family (Sun in the 12th house ruling the 12th house) and the subsequent role taken on by the women elders (Neptune as the apex planet) to handle the practical (fixed T-Square), mundane (6th house) and local affairs (3rd house) of the family (12th house).

2. The second pattern is the fear within Olivia's family of being different (Uranus conjunct the North Node in the 12th house). Yet Olivia is the one in her family who, by reaching for her own sense of individuality, causes chaos and upheaval and ultimately reshapes the family pattern. When she was young, Olivia may have enjoyed being different to her family (Uranus conjunct the Leo North Node in the 12th house). However, by her late twenties using her intuition alone becomes unsatisfactory and in order to balance this, she may have stepped into the world of ideas and concepts (Aquarius South Node). In time, with the added structure that this gives her, Olivia may find that she can step back into the world of her imagination and dreams and truly find her individuality.

Olivia's background

> I was born in Malta though my early life was lived travelling between Malta, London and Germany as my father was an officer in the British Army. When we came back to conservative Catholic Malta, I had the shock my of life; no one had a mind of their own and I felt out of place, and out of time (I was about 8 or 9 years old and I sensed this). No one understood me – only Dad, who seemed to understand what it felt like to be locked up in a mental straightjacket. I went to a convent school which I enjoyed but only because I understood there were rules which had to be followed. I followed them, made friends, but was not part of the 'in' crowd. I felt so alien here.
>
> My parents' marriage was an on/off thing for years, though Mum never showed it. When Dad was offered a job in Germany, he promised to send for us within six months, but never did. I was about 18 when he left. My plan was to leave Malta, and go back to England where I felt I'd belonged, but I couldn't leave my mother with a nervous breakdown, so I abandoned that idea.
>
> I met my sweetheart when I was 19, and life was ok – but when he decided that he was going for a career at sea, I realised that it was my karma to experience 'abandonment' of sorts by the man in my life. Through him I got in touch with

people who were into alternative thinking (chakras, healing, meditation, and so on). I became interested in Astrology at this time, and although I began to write up reports for clients (later in the 1990s), it was practically all intuitively-based information. We married in 1985 and had our first child, a boy, in 1987, followed by a girl in 1990. I was studying to become an aromatherapist in 1991 when I contracted pneumonia. After working for a few years as a professional therapist, I became bored with all the alternative stuff and decided to go to University in 1998, choosing a degree in Education because my husband suggested it (not that I don't enjoy it, but I can't say I chose teaching because that's been my life's dream).

I graduated in 2002 and have been working as a primary school teacher (though my subject is Secondary School English – of course) as my day job ever since, occasionally lecturing at Language Schools about English Methodology. This, I had decided, was a good thing, as I'd felt I needed to strengthen myself by interacting with normal [sic] people, and get a little bit grounded.

My dreams; funny area this. I'm beginning to realise that my dreams have been dashed so many times in my life that I've trained myself not to have many dreams (this is sad – and bad! I have to remedy this one). I suppose one of them is to become a good astrologer, as I really enjoy interacting with the charts. Another is to write. I think it would be nice to know if I'm doing the right thing, though having a 12th house Leo Sun, I'm never quite sure if I'm leading, or being led.

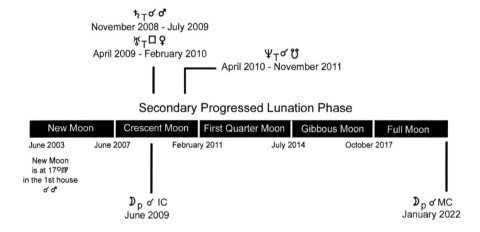

Olivia's predictive astrology

What can Olivia do to help co-create her 'netivot'?

In 2003 Olivia began a New Secondary Progressed Lunation cycle seeded at 17 degrees Virgo conjunct her natal Mars in her 1st house. This current cycle, then, is focused on what drives Olivia, how she takes action, and how she asserts her independence as part of the mastery of her craft. In mid-2009 the Secondary Progressed Moon crosses her IC and stays in her 4th house until the end of 2011, so this is a time when issues of house, home, hearth and family claim her attention, either as issues to do with mother or mothering, or via a change of residence.

Within this time period Olivia is encountering a great deal of hard work (transiting Saturn conjunct Mars) along with increased socializing, or changes to her financial situation (transiting Uranus square Venus). Given that her natal Uranus is conjunct her North Node, this could present her with insights about how she can personally reshape her inherited family pattern. This year of hard work along with social upheaval is the precursor to two years where she is again presented with the opportunity to resolve past issues (in 2010-2011 transiting Neptune conjuncts her South Node). In this period Olivia either meets someone from her past with whom she feels she has a connection spiritually, artistically or as a healer, or else through the loss in her 'tribe' of an old wise woman, Olivia finds that she is taking on that mantle. All of these possibilites can revitalise her creative, spiritual and artistic imagination.

Looking further ahead, in 2022 her Secondary Progressed Moon crosses her MC. If Olivia's goals are to become a good astrologer and writer, then these years immediately ahead of her are the times to set those goals in motion in order for her to capitalize on the potential success and reshaping of her social status in the 2020s. However, given the imminent Neptune transit of 2010-2011, it may be most useful for her to begin with this one:

1. Olivia can reshape her letters 'a', 'b' and 'o' to flush out hidden emotions and held secrets.

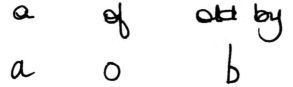

2. Olivia can then use non-lined paper to help her set her own rules.

3. She can then focus on maintaining a consistency of loops in her valley landscape letters – 'f', 'g', and 'y', including her capital 'Y'.

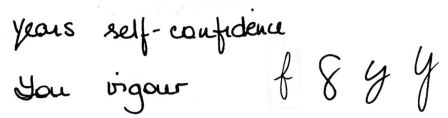

4. She can pay attention to maintaining a consistency of letter 't' cross-bars, drawing them firmly across the top of the stem evenly from left to right.

5. She can begin to make a 'bow-and-arrow' letter 'f' to bring in all three landscapes – her inspiration and imagination, her practicality and her emotions.

6. She can begin to include sweeps up into the mountains on her letters 'f', 'h', 'k', and 'l' to allow her imagination and inspiration to flourish once more.

Working slowly, making changes to one letter at a time over the course of a month before moving on to the next and doing so hand in hand with her predictive work, Olivia can begin to remodel her life within the bounds of her chart. In this way piece by piece her 'netivot' begin to reveal themselves, and as long as Olivia is open to the small changes in her life that signify shifts of attitude, she can begin to move towards her goals with greater confidence and satisfaction.

Strategy

Look back now at what you wrote in your notebook. Then use the handwriting checklist summaries from Chapters Three and Four. There will be parts of your handwriting where it is obvious that you are unwittingly expressing difficulties and issues. There will also be many positive traits and it is important to acknowledge both.

Now look at your natal chart and see if you can find where those traits, positive as well as troublesome, lie. Make a note of them.

Think carefully about your life at this time. What areas are complicated and causing you difficulty? Can you see this reflected in your handwriting? Can you also find this in the natal chart? In Chapter One I wrote of how our chart is the 'being' – what we are to begin with – but our lives and the choices we make are the 'becoming' – how we achieve our chart. I also suggested that the shape-changing or protean quality of handwriting makes it a brilliant tool and a perfect bridge to help the 'becoming'. How can you help the 'being' of your chart move to its 'becoming' through your handwriting?

Using the Secondary Progressed Lunation cycle and transits, or whatever predictive technique you find most useful, assess where you are headed in the big picture over the next ten years or so, as well as in the smaller yearly predictive work. How do your plans for yourself fit into this view? How will you begin to reshape your handwriting to ensure that those plans have the best possible support for 'becoming'?

Remember, make one small change only until you can comfortably write with that change effortlessly incorporated into your handwriting.

Work with it in conjunction with your predictive work.

Look for the small events that will enter your life which represent those changes and act on them.

8

A Guide to the Living Alphabet

What follows are examples from people's handwriting. In each example I have focused on one specific letter of the alphabet and considered the statements that letter makes about the writer's attitudes and behaviour when woven together with the other letters within that word.

A

(About). Written as a triangle, this letter 'a' contains three angles, suggesting a strong intellect and a natural sharpness of thought, as well as a probing, exploring mind, someone who generates ideas and wants to solve problems and will resist interference from others. Yet the low cross-bar on the letter 't' suggests this person sets low goals for themselves.

(That). This letter 'a' is written as a choked letter. Not only is it larger than the other letters in the plains landscape but it contains luggage on the right-hand side, suggesting the writer is withholding information from others, either personal information producing emotional distress, or intentional dishonesty. The rising cross-bar of the letter 't' at the beginning of the word shows optimism, and the cross-bar placed to the right of the letter 't' at the end of the word indicates they are good at completing projects, but may be unwilling to stretch beyond their comfort zone. However, the choked letter 'a' implies they have difficulty maintaining a clear-eyed practical focus.

This style of letter 'a' shows the writer's creativity, artistry and originality. However, it can also mean that the person is protecting themselves from past hurts or abuse.

The sharp angles of this letter 'a' indicate an intellectual approach to practical problems. However, the low cross-bar of the letter 't' suggests that this writer has little or no ambition and is angry about it (the tick on the bottom of the letter 't').

(That). The open top on this letter 'a' suggests the writer has little capacity for listening, equating garrulousness with friendliness (the undulating left side of the letter 'h') and intellect (the pointed top to the end of the letter 'h').

The use of the upper case letter 'a' amongst lower case letters indicates a person who has taste, thinks outside the box and doesn't like to be tied down. However, in this example the downward slope of the word shows mental or physical exhaustion, mirroring the word that is being written.

B

beautiful

This letter 'b' is written with an underscore connecting it with the letter next to it, suggesting a need for physical security. This is emphasized by the tight proximity of the letter 'e'. Furthermore the letter 'a' is completely encircled suggesting that the person is holding tightly onto information and thus being metaphorically strangled by that which they cannot speak, and the letter 'f' is a propellor 'f' so they unwittingly damage their best intentions at the last moment.

b

The loop of this letter 'b' shows that the person keeps the trust given to them by other people but this may also be a burden they carry.

best

This is a variation on the above. This time, however, given the forward slant of the letters, the person reaches out enthusiastically to others.

busy

Another variation. This time the compressed letters describe a contained person with inhibited self-expression.

begun

The pointed top to this letter 'b' indicates that this person takes an intellectual approach to their goals and aspirations. However, since this also forms a container, this may be a smokescreen for hidden aggression reiterated by the tick at the bottom of the letter 'g'.

November

This letter 'b' is open at its base. When oval shaped letters are open at their base, they indicate dishonesty and hypocrisy. In this case it may be to cover early emotional hurt (the letters lean to the left and the letter 'o' contains luggage), since the letters also show a combination of warmth (undulating) and intellect (angularity).

better

(Better). This letter 'b' is a variation of the above, reinforced by the retraced, rather than open, loop of the letter 'e' in the plains landscape.

This letter 'b' looks like the number '6' and suggests someone who is adept at handling money and since the letters lean to the left, this skill has been taught by the family or learnt as a result of the family's financial difficulties. Connected with the 't' bar crossed to the right of the stem, this is someone who helps other people complete their projects.

(Able). The letter 'b' and letter 'l' together resemble twin flames. This is the gesture of someone who wants to inspire and hold a flame for others spiritually. The pointed top of the letter 'l' suggests a keen and alert mind. However, the writer has placed a loop on the letter 'b' which usually carries none. This suggests that they do have ambition. However, the fear of failure means they direct their ideas along a more a spiritual pathway.

c

This letter 'c' is written as a clean letter with no hidden agendas.

This hook is enough for the person to pull on or be pulled by others' emotions. Since the letter is written in the upright position, this suggests intellectual dogmatism.

This hook is one that functions at a deeper level and connected with handwriting that slopes to the right, suggests someone who is aggressive and impatient and will not let go easily.

In this example, the hook of the letter 'c' is one that embeds itself quite deeply into the vulnerability of others. Although the letter 't' is crossed evenly at the top from left to right and slanting upwards, suggesting high ambitions and the confidence to follow through, the hook in combination with a slash 'i'-dot and the hidden luggage on the letter 'r' and the first letter 's' indicate someone with harsh opinions of other people.

171

enclose

The grappling hook on this letter 'c' reflects someone who is holding onto an excruciatingly painful experience and resolutely refuses to let it go. They have created a harmful, deeply-enduring judgmental link between themselves and another and continually relive those events in the present.

packets

This letter 'c' contains a kite pulling it back down to the ground of the writer's past. It also has a blunt end, suggesting the person takes a bludgeoning approach to situations in an attempt to break free from the past.

conversation

This letter 'c' contains a closed loop, suggesting a secret held from others about themselves.

D

d

This letter 'd' is written as a clear letter with no hidden agendas.

d d

An inflated letter 'd' stem is a storage container for an accumulation of blame and a self-sabotage shape. The more exaggerated the loop, the more it can resemble a heavy backpack of emotions which collects and festers.

made

This letter 'd' along with the letter 'o' (see 'O') contains many unspoken worries and buried concerns that this person carries around in their daily life, manifesting as an inability to confront difficult issues. Indeed they feel this so deeply that they have literally lassoed the letter 'd'. Unless they can find the means to open up and talk with someone about these fears and anxieties, they may find this results in a health issue.

mnderstand

This letter 'd' is written with a retraced stroke instead of a circle; the stem curls back on itself to the left - the past - like a scorpion's tail, suggesting someone who has been verbally attacked by their family and who is now so sensitive to criticism that they attack first. In this case, being connected with angular writing in their plains landscape, they have learnt to use a sharp intellect as a weapon.

and

This letter 'd' contains stored luggage on the left side of the letter as well as leaning to the left, indicating issues from the writer's past that continue to have a hold on them .

provided

A Greek delta 'd' can be a sign of literary interests, indicating someone who is interested in history and genealogy (the past). However, in this case it is linked with criticism (the dash 'i' dot), the inability to keep confidences (the open letter 'o') and stubbornness (the 'fist' on the right side of the letter 'o').

final

This is the 'Queen of Denial' letter 'd' found in the handwriting of those who blame others for their difficulties, yet are fearful of confrontation and defining clear boundaries about what they will and won't undertake. The leftward lean of the handwriting suggests someone who is held by the past or has encountered deep early emotional hurt resulting in protective caution. This is reinforced by the overarching letter 'f' with its desire to protect.

E

the

This letter 'e' written as a small Greek 'e', indicates the agile and responsive mind of someone with fine taste. However, in this example, coming at the end of the word and bigger than the rest of the letters, it suggests someone who seeks attention but who does not believe they have the ability to achieve their goals (the low cross-bar of the letter 't').

Euphoria

This is a far better balanced letter 'e' and the fine taste is carried across the rest of the letters through balance, spacing and shape, offering a pleasing harmony, although the 'o' is encircled.

173

enclosed A printed letter 'e' suggests a desire to stay within the bounds of habits or practices. Additionally, in this case, since all the letters are written so tightly together, there is little room for spontaneity. At the same time the convex baseline of the letter suggests someone who begins ventures with enthusiasm but lacks the vitality or drive to complete them.

the This letter 'e' is far more spontaneous and the extension at the end of the letter indicates an ability to reach out to others, to relate, socialize and share thoughts and ideas. However, whilst the retraced upstroke of the letter 't' reflects this person's pride in their accomplishments, the height of the 't' cross bar is low, and the stem has a small container indicating sensitivity to criticism, real or perceived, which may inhibit them from performing at their best.

extremely In this example, the letters diminish as they progress from beginning to end; the letter 'e' that begins it is much larger than the letter 'e' towards the end, indicating someone who runs out of energy. This may be due to the constraints that are apparent in the letter 'm' which contains retraced down strokes, a sign of control and holding back. The letter 'l' is also retraced, so this person's inspiration ('l') has been squeezed out of them.

F

sufficiently The double 'propeller f' here indicates self-sabotage. The person reaches for their goals and dreams and then unconsciously sabotages themselves at the last moment.

focused (Focused). This letter 'f' begins well but ends up being pulled back into a past situation.

 This is the highly creative, self-confident, forceful letter 'f' of someone who is used to carrying out other people's ideas instead of her own (non-existent mountain sweep) and who, out of frustration and feeling trapped, unconsciously uses her emotions to undermine or destroy her efforts (half propeller 'f').

(Of). This letter 'f 'shows someone who feels trapped into serving others and who has created and now holds onto a waterhole of emotions which have no outlet.

This letter 'f' reflects someone who is constantly doing things for other people and claims nothing for themselves. Underlying this is a desperate longing for the acknowledgment of their special gifts. However, through fear or a sense of inadequacy, they have never appropriately expressed their needs or desires.

This letter 'f' is focused almost entirely in the realm of imagination and inspiration, so the person is able to reach easily into that world but they may not necessarily contain the practicality to make those dreams a reality. Indeed the lower part of the letter is retraced.

(Fine). This letter 'f' is another form of propeller, this time with the addition of angles in the valley landscape of emotions and instinct. So not only does this person sabotage their plans at the last moment, they also intellectualise their feelings as a way of justifying their position.

This letter 'f' indicates someone who is fearful of the future and who builds a wall in front of their dreams so they will not have to venture forward. The person has repeated this movement in both the capital 'F' and lowercase. The long detached bar of the letter 't' suggests an ambitious, enthusiastic person, with a protective attitude who is better at completing other people's projects than their own.

Here the letter 'f' forms a 'cat's cradle' in the valley landscape of emotions. This indicates someone who is highly sensitive to emotional criticism and who may appear indecisive and repressed. With no sweep up into their mountain landscape, this is someone whose projects are so emotionally entangled that they feel unable to move ahead with their goals. This is reinforced by the lack of detail indicated by the missing 'i' dots and the knotted letter 't'.

The central plains landscape of this letter 'f' contains excess luggage (see case study 'Lydia' chapter 6).

G

This letter 'g' is the symbol of a highly fluid, creative and original thinker, one who considers their profession their life and vocation and brings distinction and uniqueness to it.

Unlike the 'g' above, this creative letter 'g' begins with a fully encircled piece of luggage, so all of this person's creativity has to be filtered through self-protection.

(Imagine). This is a highly-stylised letter 'g', writen as the letter 'e' with an extension into the valley landscape, suggesting an unusual combination of imagination and thinking.

This letter 'g' with its full loop in the valley landscapes indicates a rich emotional life and a high degree of sensual and sexual needs.

Both these letter 'g's contain creativity but the writer has stopped themselves from completing the letter, either due to constraint by an emotional family issue or through fear of expressing their creativity.

This letter 'g' ends as an open hook, suggesting hidden emotional undercurrents and a degree of immaturity. This is reiterated in the slash 'i' dot and the way the letters wrap around each other for support.

This letter 'g' contains hidden luggage on the right side of the letter and a simple shaft stabbing into the valley landscape, suggesting a mistrust of emotions.

This letter 'g' with its miniscule foray into the valley landscape suggests this person has a tremendous fear of their emotions, along with a degree of impotence.

H

cheer

This letter 'h' suggests someone who allows themselves to explore the undiscovered terrain of their imagination. However, the angles in the letter indicate the person relies on their intellect to inspire them.

husk

(Husk). This letter 'h' indicates someone who approaches their goals and dreams with an objective mind and a practical approach. The letters are rhythmic and measured and indicate rational planning.

whole

This letter 'h' also implies a practical and straightforward approach to life. However, unlike the example above, the letters contain varying slants and an uneven rhythm, suggesting a restless mind and nervous energy.

thank

When part of a letter creates the one that follows, it is called a ligature and it represents a fluid thinker, someone with a flexible attitude who copes well in stressful situations. However, in this case there is no mountain sweep on the letter 'h' and it is instead written as a retraced letter (as is the letter 'k') which suggests someone who feels trapped in some way. The part of the letter 'h' written in the plains landscape is written with a pull away stroke, meaning this writer naturally pulls away from old conditioning. However, the tall mountain landscape and reduced plains landscape indicates that the writer feels a strain between their everyday practical and social world and their goals and ambitions, like a stretched elastic band.

the

This letter 'h' is written with a left hand slant, suggesting someone who is held by the past. The letter itself looks more like the letter 'n' than an 'h', without height nor sweep into the mountains, signifying a lack of personal inspiration.

the

This letter 'h' is tall and lean. The writer has a strong imaginative life and the rightward slant indicates someone who seeks a challenge. However, in the practical plains landscape the letter is retraced and pulled in, indicating that this writer represses their spontaneity and blocks their creativity, severely limiting their capacity to manifest their ideas. They are, in effect, pregnant with dreams and creative potential but are far too fearful to allow those dreams to manifest. This is reinforced by the letter 't' crossed relatively high but still below the top of the letter, suggesting they set their goals at a level they feel they can reach for fear of failure in reaching for what they truly want. As well, the second letter is written higher than the first, indicating self-consciousness, fear of social embarrassment and an apprehensive approach to the world.

I

A capital 'I' with serifs suggests someone with cultured interests and who is confident and independent. In this case with the right slant, the person is also enthusiastic and outgoing.

This narrow simple capital 'I' suggests someone who is confident and independent, who wants to be seen as they are and who maintains a clear mind.

This capital 'I' with serifs off the stem of the letter, containing flicks and leaning to the left suggests poor self-esteem and over-compensation.

This capital 'I' written like the number nine suggests someone whose image in the world is dependent upon money.

This angular capital 'I' suggests someone who is critical and hostile, particularly of themselves.

This capital 'I' looks like a person curled up in themselves and is a protective statement, the desire to be cared for and nurtured.

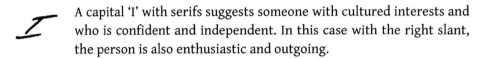

This capital 'I' with its connection to the following word suggests someone who does not want to lose the continuity of their thoughts by lifting their pen from the paper, as well as someone who works well under pressure. It is also written with an underscore connecting it to the next letter, suggesting a need for physical security.

J

The letter 'j' can be read like the letter 'i' with regard to the dot above it and the letter 'y' when it comes to the flow into the valley.

enjoyed

In this letter 'j' the dot is placed to the right of the letter and high, meaning this person is future-orientated and enthusiastic. However, it is also jagged indicating anger or resentment to do with their purpose and ambition. The full loop suggests a vivid imagination, although the slight point indicates tension and that the person could have a sharp tongue and critical attitude.

judge

In this letter 'j' the dot is placed to the right of the letter and close to it, meaning this person is future-orientated but cautious, and written as a slash suggests some form of annoyance. Since the loop ends before it can cross from the valley landscape into the practical area of their life, it suggests someone who stops short of allowing themselves emotional fulfilment.

enjoyable

In this letter 'j' the dot is placed high and directly above the letter, meaning this person pays attention to their surroundings and has good powers of concentration. The dot is a dash and hence contains some irritation.

joy

This letter 'j' is formed with a straight line downward indicating that the writer is independent and confident. However, the heavy pressure, the forceful dot, and the small tick-like stroke on the end of the letter 'y' indicate a degree of emotional hostility.

joy

The open and wide curve of the stem in the valley landscape of this letter 'j' indicates someone who is gentle and loving and who may also be emotionally immature. The falling away of the letter 'y' suggests mental or physical exhaustion, in which case this word may well be a trigger word, as the way it is written is opposite to its meaning.

judging

In this letter 'j' the dot is placed to the left, indicating someone who lacks self-confidence and is trapped by the past in some way. This is reinforced by the leftward slant of the writing.

K

This letter 'k' is written as a stem with a buckle, indicating someone who likes intimacy, and the extended end to the letter suggests someone who reaches out to others.

(Works). This letter 'k' is written more as a wide, soft letter 'w' bookended by two loops, suggesting contrived friendliness.

This letter 'k' is open on the underside of the letter where the buckle usually goes through the stem, written more like the letter 'h', suggesting a degree of impracticality and a fear of intimacy.

(Kind). This letter 'k', written like the letters 'l' and 'i', suggests someone who is emotionally disconnected from others.

In this rather unusual form of the letter 'k' there is no mountain sweep, and the movement back to the practical plains landscape does not form a buckle but a pointed angle. This suggests that when it comes to relationships there are few dreams or aspirations (no mountain sweep). Instead there are hidden issues (the lassoed loop on the left) and they have learnt to approach intimacy and forming commitments (the buckle) using their intellect (the pointed angle).

This capital letter 'k' in the midst of a word suggests someone who in some way defies the norms of society and prefers to live outside the mainstream when it comes to connecting with others.

L

This letter 'l' is written in a highly simplified manner, suggesting an agile mind with no hidden agendas.

This letter 'l' also has no hidden agendas, although the left slant indicates someone who is guarded and defensive.

This letter 'l' is another variation of someone with no hidden agendas, but who may be reclusive, and the backward hook of the vally loop of the letter 'y' reinforces this grip from the past.

This letter 'l' on the other hand, with its right hand slant, indicates someone who seeks challenges in their life.

These letter 'l's, with their emphasized slant to the right, indicate someone who is enthusiastic and eager and who may also be reactive and impatient.

This letter 'l' contains an upward sweep into the mountain landscape. In letters where such movements are appropriate, such as this one, they represent someone who finds their own inspiration in life. The fact that the two letter 't's that follow also contain loops on their stems indicates someone who is sensitive and who takes criticism to heart.

The sweep on this letter 'l' looks like a heart, as does the letter 'e'. Indeed 'life' turned out to be a trigger word, for in the last few years this woman had experienced the death of her closest friend and the suicide of her ex-husband.

M

This letter 'm' is written without adornment, suggesting simple tastes, someone who allows space and time for their own thoughts and is also willing to listen to others. The letter 'p', however, does contain some emotional baggage.

When the right-hand side of the letter 'm' is raised above the left it indicates an inferiority complex. The writer's ego is lower than the image they have of the other person and so they are dependent on the other person's opinions. It also shows that the writer needs to get their own way. If this is thwarted, verbal hostility may often lead to regret. In this example the way the letter 'm' is written looks like clenched teeth, without spaces between the down strokes, indicating the writer is fearful of giving free rein to their originality.

181

information

This letter 'm' is also written without spaces between the down strokes, a gesture that inhibits creative expression and spontaneity. It also indicates a protective trait, a desire to control their practical world at the expense of creative freedom. It is not surprising to see that the right hand side of the letter is taller than the left, as this movement adds aggression and temper and the person's need to get their own way.

something

This letter 'm' is the 'gritted teeth m', a more extreme case of the example above. The writer is held by pressures around them in day to day life, unable to express their resourcefulness and natural creativity. The dash 'i' dot and the letter 'g' which ends as an open hook reinforces the repressed anger.

me

(Me). This letter 'm' with its initial retraced down stroke designates someone who is partially held by the needs of others. However, the second half of the letter is written as a pull away stroke, as if the writer explodes out of the pressures placed upon them by the past. Furthermore the angularity indicates clarity of thinking, as well as a possible brusqueness of manner.

empower

This unadorned letter 'm' implies someone with simple tastes. However, since the middle stroke does not touch the ground of the plains landscape, there is a lack of practicality influenced by the past (leftward lean), and a lack of confidence and a dependency on the opinions of others (right hand hump higher than the left) .

am

This letter 'm' also shows an inferiority complex. However, this time as the letters are written upright, it is in the area of responsibility. The rounded printing shows the person yields easily to others and hence can be imposed upon and readily influenced.

women

This letter 'm' looks like a mountain that is collapsing in on itself and being propped up from both sides. This suggests a person who is torn, who cannot decide whether they want to live in the past, present, or future. The container of the letter 'o' adds the burden of keeping a secret.

N

garden

This letter 'n' has a clear separation from its first downstroke and denotes someone who lives their own life and makes their own decisions with no hidden agendas.

not

The straight, rigid, inflexible introductory mark of this letter 'n' is called a resentment stroke. The length of the mark, this is made by someone who unconsciously projects emotional anger and bitterness from deep within their past into their everyday world.

Beginning

The angles on the letter 'n's denote someone who uses their incisive intellect, analytical and critical skills in their work. They take in information quickly and can readily retrieve data from memory. In contrast, when letters are written with cavities where there are none it suggests information leaks away. In this example, the open base of the capital 'B' and the open tops of the letters 'g' means the person shows little respect for confidences and may therefore be untrustworthy with personal information.

Consultation

The rounded top of this letter 'n' indicates friendliness, openness and a kind heart. Added to this, the separation of the letters suggests this is someone who is open to the ideas of others.

Congratulations

In contrast, this letter 'n' is part of writing that looks like tangled wool, written by someone who is not only not open to other people's ideas but may not even hear their own inner thoughts, since the word is written without the pen even being lifted from the paper. The right slant which suggests enthusiasm also indicates impatience, the letters 'o' are lassoed and contain luggage, and the creative letter 'g' has a hook on it. The underlying implications of these gestures belie the word's face value.

understand Both of these letter 'n's suggest inhibition and a tie to the past and the fact that letters that would normally sweep up into the mountains all sit in the practical plains emphasizes the functional dominance of this person's everyday world.

aunt (Aunt). This letter 'n' looks almost the same as the letter 'u'. This garlanded letter 'n' with an angular tip suggests this is someone who wants to reach out to others but also wishes to boast about their intellect.

O

one The straight, rigid, inflexible introductory mark of this letter 'o' is called a resentment stroke. Since it begins deep within the valley landscape, this suggests there is a great deal of emotional anger and bitterness from deep within their past. This is compounded by the confidential information this person is holding for other people.

o Whilst the upright stance of the letters indicates clear thinking and self-confidence, this letter 'o' is a variation on the above.

o The container on the top of this letter 'o' is that of someone who keeps confidences. However, this particular movement cuts the top third of the letter 'o' suggesting that, in doing so, it is choking them.

to A letter 'o' that is open at the top suggests someone who is open, frank and talkative and who may show little respect for confidences.

apologies Both 'o' letters here are entirely scooped up, indicating that the person is holding tightly onto a secret, living in such fear of discovery that it is repressing or inhibiting their behaviour. Furthermore the writer does not lift their pen from the page, so they barricade themselves from hearing other people's ideas and even their own inner thoughts.

paramount

The letter 'o' in this handwriting has been written above the line, suggesting a creative and individualistic approach to life.

good

These letter 'o's are open on the left hand side indicating issues from the past which erode the present. As a result this person may be obsessive and fearful and cover it by being acquisitive and egotistical.

P

probably

This letter 'p' has a full round circle, indicating clarity of focus, even though it slants to the left, indicating reclusive tendencies.

spiritual

This letter 'p' is formed with an elliptical circle, suggesting an imaginative and artistic component to this person's practical world. This is emphasized by the mountain sweep of the letter 'l' and the precise placement of the 'i' dots, suggesting they pay attention to details.

people

This letter 'p' is open at the base, suggesting some form of dishonesty and duplicity. Focused mainly into the practical plains area of their life, it is coupled with a lassoed letter 'o' (holding onto a secret that is strangling them) and a retraced letter 'l' (inspiration bound by chains).

helpful

In this word the right slant indicates sociability. However, this letter 'p' has a cellar of trapped emotion at its base, indicating the person is keeping a secret or witholding information. When this is connected with the hook at the beginning of the letter 'h' indicating being hooked to the past, the letter 'f' suggesting the person is following someone else's pattern, and the retraced upstroke of the final letter 'l' suggesting unfulfilled dreams, it reveals someone who is caught in the web of an unconscious pattern.

disappointment

This letter 'p' contains deep cellars of trapped emotions on the left hand side of the letter and at the base of it.

185

Q

quality

This letter 'q', written as a letter 'g', contains luggage on the right hand side and forms a soft angle of completion in the valley landscape, suggesting someone who intellectualizes their emotions or is caught in emotionally-triangulated situations.

quality

This letter 'q' is written as a crossed stem in the valley landscape. This short or arrested stem suggests they are afraid to trust their instincts, so block any messages they receive at that level.

quality

This letter 'q', written as a full loop and slanted to the right, reveals someone with full-bodied instincts and emotions.

quality

This letter 'q' is written as a full loop with the tail pulled back to the left in the valley landscape, suggesting accumulated and incomplete unconscious emotions pulling the person back into their past.

quality

This letter 'q' is written like a letter 'f', with the loop reaching deeply into the person's valley landscape indicating strong security instincts and a predominant sensuality.

quality

This letter 'q' is written as an unadorned short stem with a angle flick to the right, indicating a degree of aggression.

cheque

This letter 'q' is written with a secondary container in its center, implying a secret, and leaning heavily to the right suggests the person is over-dependent on others. The hook in the letter 'c' implies they are holding onto their past, and a retraced stroke in the mountain sweep of the letter 'h', suggests the person's inspiration has been squeezed out of them. As a trigger word, it suggests that this person ties themselves in knots over financial matters.

R

recollection

This rounded letter 'r' indicates sociability and friendliness, even though the letter 'o' shows that the writer plays their cards close to their chest and withholds information.

regards

(Regards). This letter 'r' is much more reserved, indicated by the leftward slant and the rigid adherence of the letter to the stem. In combination with the encircled letter 'g', the container on the left hand side of the letter 'a' and the inflated letter 'd' stem, this suggests someone who feels weighed down with secrets and information by which they feel stifled or strangled. This is in contradiction to the open top of the letter 'a' which denotes garrulousness.

your

This letter 'r', with its forward slant and upward movement separate from its stem, points to someone with energy and excitement.

room

This letter 'r', with its sharp angle connecting it to the following letter, denotes someone who thinks logically and has good planning and organizing abilities. The two letter 'o's that follow both contain trapped emotions connected with a person's daily life and suggest that this person is withholding information from other people. Indeed the art that is created is of two eyes that watch, or someone wearing spectacles. Both these traits together suggest anxiety and inner tension.

referring

The two letter 'r's together in the middle of this word indicate someone who is open to ideas and information, emphasized by the space between 'referr' and 'ing'. However, the self-sabotage propeller 'f' unconsciously works against this person's plans.

respect

The writer of this letter 'r' is not at all interested in listening to other people's ideas and in combination with the cross bar of the letter 't' drawn at the top and with firm pressure, it suggests someone who is self-assured and opinionated, whilst the open letter 'p' at the base suggests some form of dishonesty and duplicity.

nigour

(Vigour). This letter 'r' at the end of the word completes in the mountain landscape with a knot suggesting unfinished business.

S

special

This simple letter 's' denotes someone who is constructive in their thinking.

positive

This letter 's' holds luggage at the top and the bottom of its shape, giving a sense of the person being handcuffed and in leg-irons. This forwards-backwards movement is referred to by Vimala Rodgers as 'Miles of Lace'. When written across or down the page this movement acts as a stress-reduction exercise as it slows a person down and reverses forward-moving energy. When a letter 's' is shaped in this way it acts as a brake, arresting the person's progress.

present

This letter 's' in the centre of this word is shaped like a swan and represents elegance and originality.

spoke

This letter 's' is also shaped in the swan position but this one carries extra luggage under its wing, causing it to look more like the number '8', suggesting someone who is powerful, confident and materially successful. However, since this is also contains luggage, it suggests that this person's hidden concerns may involve money.

person

This letter 's' looks like a letter 'o' that is open on the left hand side, so it is likely that this person may be dealing with issues from the past which affect the present.

essential

This letter 's' suggest friendliness and sociability. However, the downward slope of the writing also suggests mental or physical exhaustion.

T

A looped vertical stem is another place to store hidden issues. This indicates misplaced ambition, seeking achievement and credibility through an unyielding pathway, or goals and ambitions which have been thwarted, resulting in disappointment.

Wherever handwriting produces a knot, it reveals a person with persistence. These two examples of triangulated letter 't's indicate people who resent interference, and can become aggressive if questioned.

The letter 't' in this handwriting shows ambition and a desire to stretch for and achieve their highest goals, although the slight lean to the left shows a degree of introversion and reserve.

The letter 't' in this handwriting, on the other hand, shows the same ambition but now with optimism (the upwards incline of the cross-bars) and a willingness to share experiences (rightward slant).

These two examples of 't' cross-bars extending over the following letters suggest over-caring behaviour. The concave scoop, however, acts as a bowl in the mountain region, holding onto stagnant dreams and goals.

A ligature is a unifying link or bond joining one part of a letter to another, the most common being the 't' with 'h'. It indicates a fluid thinker with an agile mind and a flexible attitude who copes well under stressful conditions.

However, when the cross-bar forms a concave scoop, then it acts as a bowl in the practical plains and does not allow plans to come to fruition.

fact

This letter 't' written as a flick or tick indicates someone with a quick mind, impatient to reach their goals and who wants to finish quickly. Hence they may also be aggressive and have a short temper. When combined with the day-dreaming letter 'f' and the low placement of the flick on the stem of the letter 't', it suggests someone who feels under the thumb of others and is resentful of it.

U

you

The intrinsic shape of the letter 'u' is the rounded shape of networking, socializing and relating. Although the letter 'o' in this example is entirely lassoed and the letter 'u' at the end of the word is smaller in size than the other letters, the letter 'u' is written with confidence in the upright position and with the rounded shape of a friendly gesture.

You

This letter 'u' is willing to reach out to others, denoted by the upturned and open ending. However, the letter 'o' contains confidential information.

your

The spacing between this letter 'o and letter 'u' is much wider, suggesting someone who is much more spontaneous and open in attitude to others.

Australia

Angularity in the letter 'u' denotes a strong resistance to friendliness. This letter 'u' is verging on angular. When this is connected with the slash 'i' dot, the 'flick' or 'tick' letter 't', the container in the letter 's' and the encircled final letter 'a', this is someone who unconsciously resents infringement of their time and space.

about

(About). This letter 'u' is angular in shape, and there is friendliness in the undulating letters and a clear letter 'o' without any agendas. The cross-bar of the letter 't' to the right of the stem suggests they complete projects. However, the constricted letter 'b' suggest this person finds it arduous at times to have to socialize.

V

private

This is a clean letter 'v' with no hidden agendas. As a natural angle, it shows the person approaches their daily life from an intellectual point of view.

very

This curved letter 'v' leans to the right indicating amiability and friendliness. However the downward slope of the word suggests fatigue.

every

This letter 'v' contains luggage on the right hand side.

very

This letter 'v' leans to the left, pulling the person back towards their past in some way.

tentatively

This letter 'v' stands upright in a word that is written with a rightward lean. As well, it is written almost as a letter 'u'. This confusion or indecision around direction and shape will reflect confusion or indecision in the person.

gallivanting

This letter 'v' is written with the right side higher than the left, suggesting a slight sense of inferiority.

W

which

The letter 'w' can be written as rounded or angular. In this example, the letter 'w' has luggage on the right hand side, which suggests the person stores secrets and restricted information for other people. When coupled with the retraced upstrokes on the letter 'h's, indicating that this person's inspiration has been squeezed out of them, and handwriting that is written directly on the line, this suggests someone who has opted to live by rules which no longer nourish them but who has no idea how to change their circumstances.

When a letter 'w' contains angles it indicates a sharp mind. This writer has balanced intellect with easygoing friendliness in their letter 'w'. However, the hook embedded into the circle of the letter 'd' and the half propeller 'f' indicate someone who feels irritated by having to be in service to others.

(Wish). This letter 'w' denotes someone who wants to balance intellect with sociability but the leftward slant, along with the protective sweep of the letter 's' in its connection with the letter 'h', indicates they prefer seclusion.

This letter 'w' is another example of the desire to balance intellect with ease of social networking.

This is a simple, friendly letter 'w'. Whilst recognizing that letter 'p' is open at the base and the letter 'o' contains emotional baggage, when someone writes a letter 'w' in this way what you see is what you get.

X

Historically when someone was not literate they used an 'x' to sign their name on documents, so the letter 'x' has the additional implication of identity. However, whilst the letter 'x' is written as two separate strokes crossing each other, the left or second stroke can move either towards the valley landscape, hence towards the body and its emotions, or else towards the mountains and inspiration.

In this letter 'x', the first stroke is a continuation of the letter 'e' and so it is retraced, meaning the pen travels back over part of the letter and so traps the person in their past.

This letter 'x' is written with one cross bar curved across the other, covering or protecting the self, body or identity.

(is experienced). This letter 'x' is written as a half bow moving back on itself like an infinity sign and as such forms a container on the right hand side.

This letter 'x' is written with the left hand side as a concave curve with the cross bar through it, like a bow and arrow, suggesting someone who aims for their target. This is reinforced by the long upward slant of the letter 't' cross bar.

This letter 'x' is written with a tick on the end of the left hand cross bar, suggesting resentment, and the diminishing size of the word suggests fatigue.

This letter 'x' is written with a knot on the left hand side, indicating persistence, stubbornness, and a desire to have their own way.

This letter 'x' is written as two half circles back to back with each other, rather than two lines crossing, suggesting two opposing forces in the self-identity. As well the left hand half-circle forms a closed loop of hidden secrets.

Y

The backward hook on this letter 'y' is often called a 'grasping claw' and indicates strong family ties. It can also be the sign of someone who hoards emotions, as it sits in the valley landscape. In this case linked with a backward slant, it suggests someone who is tied to or hooked into emotional family issues.

This is a similar scenario, although the 'claw' is softer than the above example. However in this case there are two 'claws' – on the capital 'J' in the plains landscape and one on the letter 'y' in the valley landscape. This suggests the writer is pulled back to their family through practical and emotional matters. Given the lack of space between letters, they prefer to keep their own counsel and do not allow others' ideas to infiltrate their thinking.

The large full loop suggests strong emotions, instincts, and sensual drives.

The shortened end of the letter 'y' dipping only briefly into the writer's valley landscape indicates a quick grasp of situations unhampered by emotions.

The extreme rightward slant of this writing indicates someone who is highly gregarious and enthusiastic or else impatient. The protracted end of the letter 'y' deep into the valley landscape also indicates independence, physical energy and good organizing abilities.

Z

The sweep down into the valley landcape of this letter 'z' contains a triangle, suggesting that, intentionally or unintentionally, this person always finds themselves involved in emotionally-triangulated situations.

The valley sweep of this letter 'z' is heavy with excess activity, although the upward slant of the word indicates optimism.

In this example, the squared practical plains part of the letter 'z' suggests a mind closed to new thoughts and ideas, and the miniscule foray into the valley landscape indicates someone who is fearful of encountering their instincts and emotions.

amazement In contrast with the tight, retraced downstrokes of the beginning of the letter 'z' and the letters 'm' and 'n', suggesting the person feels trapped in the daily routines of their life, the valley sweep of this letter 'z' is soft and full, indicating that they are emotionally well-balanced.

These letter 'z's are all written in the practical plains landscape, focusing on the mundane practicalities:

amazement *amazement*

amazement *amazement*

Trauma

Extremes of handwriting are always of interest, for they show the edges of the bell-curve, the degree to which people can sustain trauma and still emerge with a productive and fruitful life. The handwriting will also be reflective of difficult circumstances suggested by aspects in their natal chart.

'Xena'

Xena[1] was born in 1957. She developed diabetes mellitus type '1' when she was twelve years old and had to learn to medicate herself with between four and five injections a day, a practice that continued for thirty years. In April 2000 this changed when she began to manage the diabetes with an insulin pump. In her words, 'it has transformed my life'.

Xena begins her correspondence high on the page indicating familiarity with the recipient. Whilst the margins are narrow, they are well-balanced. She writes her letters in an upright position indicating independence, self-confidence and a willingness to take on positions of responsibility. It also suggests that she has learnt to work well under pressure, perhaps the quality that helped her navigate the pain. Her personal pronoun capital 'I' is clear and simple, showing that she

---

1. Xena appears as a case study in my book *Life After Grief* and has given her permission for her handwriting to be used in this book.

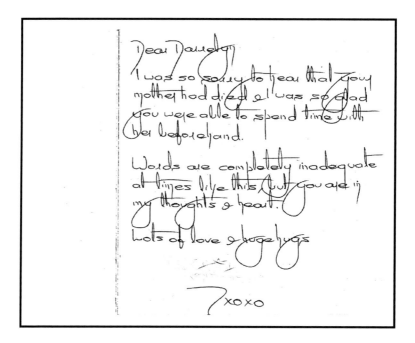

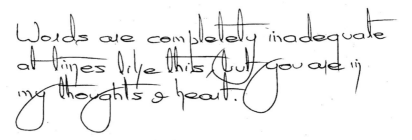

wishes to be seen as she is, although it is slightly dwarfed by the heights of the letters 't' and 'h', indicating some insecurity.

However, her handwriting is dominated by the long loops of emotional pain in the letters 'g' and 'y', communicating the extreme emotional stress under which her body has been placed for so long; the long valley trails to her letters 'h', 'm' and 'n'; and the 'flames of hope' in the mountain landscapes of her letters 'b', 'd', 'h', 'l' and 't', indicating someone who wants to inspire and hold a flame for others spiritually. The hooks on the ends of her letter 's' indicate that she feels she has suffered at the hands of others and has learned to defend herself from blame and stinging verbal attacks. All of this notwithstanding, Xena is a successful yoga teacher and astrology teacher and since 1998 has been in a long-term committed relationship.

Douglas'

Douglas is in his late fifties and came to me as a client. He has given me his permission for his handwriting to be used in this book. Douglas describes himself in this way: 'I have had the rare job of "professional mental patient" for decades, am fully in remission i.e. completely sane on medication, and wanting to leave psychiatry behind.'

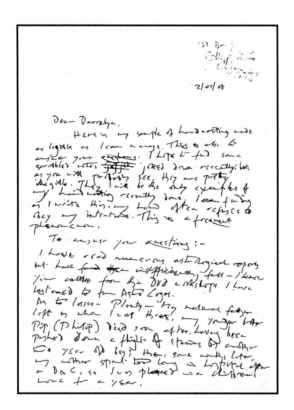

Douglas' handwriting is balanced on the page. He shows respect for the recipient by the wide margin at the top, and the narrow lower margin suggests that he wants to communicate many ideas. There is a balance of spacing between his words, indicating someone who is resourceful and creative, and a balance of spacing between the lines, indicating clear thinking, an ability to organize, motivate and maintain drive towards a goal without being diverted. His unadorned capital 'I' shows that he wishes to be seen as he actually is, and his letter 'e' indicates a quick, cultured, responsive mind. The lines begin to slope downwards in the lower half of the page as he describes his past losses. However, the dominant characteristic is the erratic formation and direction of the letters, with the letter 'd' on the one hand pulling him back into the past in terms of his dreams and goals and the letter 'q' sweeping him forward to the future emotionally. Douglas writes: 'I am finding as I write this my hand often refuses to obey my intentions. This is a frequent phenomenon.'

Alana

Alana was the subject of a mini-documentary film that I produced and directed in 1998 contrasting two women's experiences of childhood trauma. Alana suffered ritual abuse from birth until the age of eight in a trans-generational satanic coven in New Zealand. She was twenty-six years old when I made the film and at that time was working in a responsible position in a local government centre. The relationship she had been in for some time ended shortly after the film was made.

Alana's handwriting slants to the right, indicting someone who seeks challenge, is sociable and works well with people and who may also be emotionally reactive and impatient. Her handwriting hugs the left hand margin, indicating a highly insecure person whose fears stem from early life experiences. Furthermore it is written on lined paper and she writes on the lines showing that she prefers guidelines in her life and follows rules and regulations to the letter.

However, the dominant characteristic is that the writing is disturbed, or tortured, in some way, with overwritten letters, concealed luggage and erratic changes in writing quality from word to word.

9

Writing Your Future

The present... emails, SMS, word processed documents, and pens

This is the end of the book but my aim is that it is the beginning of the journey for you. By now I hope you have recognized just how much you still use pen, paper and ink and, more importantly, that the marriage of this inexpensive tool with your own hand creates one of the most powerful instruments you possess for bringing change into your life.

Using the questions at the end of Chapter Seven, assess for yourself what you see in your handwriting that hadn't been obvious before you began this journey of AstroGraphology. Correlating this with your natal chart, what new shapes would you need to make in your handwriting to help resolve current issues?

Now consider your long and short term plans and how you can use your predictive work in combination with changes to your handwriting to bring your plans to fruition. Write them in your handwriting book now.

Handwriting means active participation

Whether scratched or scrawled, inscribed with thought or jotted in haste, the words we write are powerful and meaningful to us. They contain our energy and whether we acknowledge it or not, they speak to us of our inner life and how we manifest that in our outer existence. Here are two cases in point to show you what I mean.

The first was via an email sent to me recently by a friend, Katya, who was intrigued by the idea of AstroGraphology. Twelve months ago she decided to change her letter 't'. Six months later she ended her difficult four year relationship and within a few months was in the First Fine Careless Rapture with a new man, Daniel. Katya recently gained this insight:

I was writing out Daniel's text messages because my phone memory was full and they are really special to me - I couldn't just delete them. They reflect the short and intense period when our relationship developed extremely quickly, and reading them back was like reading a diary. I decided to write them into a nice book I had bought for the purpose and make it into a kind of journal. What really struck me was that I was writing his thoughts but in my handwriting, and it felt very strange. My handwriting isn't smooth, flowing, or especially nice to look at even at the best of times, and I noticed it became quite disjointed and jumpy when I was writing the nice, complimentary things he was saying in his texts, reflecting the way I feel slightly uneasy when people compliment me, I guess. I also realised that I have been trying very hard to make my writing reflect how happy he makes me feel in an attempt to overcome old insecurities - but it is really hard! However much I sit and relax and imagine the words flowing beautifully out of the pen, I find my hand suddenly jolts and the word I have just written looks awful. This is a real journey for me - thank you!

The second instance involved a client, Beth, who was about to go overseas. As her partner was having a birthday whilst she was away, Beth ordered a gift through the internet and asked the company to include a card with a message. However, the company was incredibly efficient and the gift arrived before Beth left. Beth and her partner both work from home and they receive many deliveries as part of their daily routines. Since there was nothing on the box to indicate otherwise, Beth's partner began to open it and immediately realized it was a gift. Beth explains what happened next:

I seized the box and took it away to gift wrap it and in so doing, saw the card I had asked to be included inside. Now I have encountered instances in the past where companies include cards with messages, such as when sending flowers to someone in hospital, and I have seen the end result when I have been to visit the recipient of the gift. The company either word-processes the message or hand prints it and the message is usually generic, 'Wishing you a speedy recovery,' and so on. But my message was fairly personal - and this card was handwritten. The sight of my personal message in someone else's handwriting - and handwriting that was full of PROBLEMS - was too much. I had to shred the card. I couldn't even keep it as an example to show you. Luckily I could then write my own card in my own handwriting and place it with the gift. This whole incident was hugely insightful for me as to how much the words we write in our own handwriting reflect us and who we are.

As your handwriting changes, so your life and your 'netivot' will become apparent to you. As you change your handwriting you will learn a great deal about yourself. Be prepared to honour what you find.

Bibliography

Amend, Karen and Ruiz, Mary S. (1980) *Handwriting Analysis: The Complete Basic Book*, North Hollywood: Newcastle Publishing Co.

Armbrester, Margaret England and Miyazawa, Jiro M. (1993) *Samuel Ullman and 'Youth': The Life, the Legacy*, Tuscaloosa: University of Alabama Press.

Baxandall, Michael. (1988) *Painting and Experience in Fifteenth-Century Italy*, Oxford: Oxford University Press.

Beck, John. (2000) *Collected papers on handwriting movements and Jungian graphology*, Gerrards Cross: British Institute of Graphologists.

Brady, Bernadette. (1992) *The Eagle and The Lark: A Textbook of Predictive Astrology*, York Beach: Samuel Weiser.

————. (2006) *Astrology; a place in chaos*, Bournemouth: The Wessex Astrologer.

Branston, Barry. (1991) *Graphology Explained*, York Beach: Samuel Weiser Inc.

Cameron, Ellen. (1989) *An Introduction to Graphology*, Wellingborough: The Aquarian Press.

Cazden, Joanna. (2007) *How to Take Care of Your Voice: The Lifestyle Guide for Singers and Talkers*, Burbank: Booklocker.com.

Cohen, Frits and Wander, Daniel. (1993) *Handwriting Analysis at Work*, London: Thorsons.

Colton, R.H. and Casper J.K. (1990) *Understanding Voice Problems*, Baltimore: Williams and Wilkins.

Crépieux-Jamin, Jules. (1929) *Abc De La Graphologie*, 2 vols, Paris: Alcan.

Drews, Robert. (1993) *The End of the Bronze Age: Changes in Warfare and the Catastrophe ca. 1200 BC*, Princeton: Princeton University Press.

Engle, Joel. (1980) *Handwriting Analysis Self-Taught*, Amsterdam: Elsevier.

Furth, Gregg M. (1989) *The Secret World of Drawings: A Jungian Approach to Healing through Art*, Inner City Books: New York.

Galilei, Galileo. (2001). *Dialogue Concerning the Two Chief World Systems, Ptolemaic and Copernican*. Original edition, 1632. Translated by S. Drake. Edited by S. J. Gould (New York: The Modern Library).

Garcia, Joseph. (1999) *Sign with Your Baby*, Seattle: Northlight Communications.

Gardner, Ruth. (1991) *The Truth About Graphology*, Woodbury: Llewellyn Worldwide.

Gunzburg, Darrelyn. (2004) *Life After Grief: An Astrological Guide to Dealing with Loss*, Bournemouth: The Wessex Astrologer.

Heraclitus. (2001) *Fragments*, Translated by Brooks Haxton, London: Penguin Books.

Hood, William. 'Saint Dominic's Manners of Praying: Gestures in Fra Angelico's Cell Frescoes at San Marco', *The Art Bulletin* 68, no. 2, (1986) pp.195-206.

Jacoby, Hans J. (1940) *Changes of Character produced by Religious Conversions, as shown in Changes of Handwriting*, Guild Lecture. no. 6, London: Guild of Pastoral Psychology.

Jakobsen, Roman and Waugh, Linda R. (1987) *The Sound Shape of Language*, Bloomington: University of Indiana Press.

Jones, Alexander (ed). (1968) *The Jerusalem Bible*, Reader's Edition, Garden City, New York: Doubleday & Company, Inc.

Kaplan, Aryeh. (1997) *Sefer Yetzirah, the Book of Creation, Revised Edition*, San Francisco: Red Wheel/Weiser.

Kendon, Adam. (1972) 'Some Relationships between Body Motion and Speech'. In *Studies in Dyadic Communication*, edited by Siegman A. and Pope B., pp.177-210, New York: Pergammon Press.

Ladefoged, P. (1974) *Elements of Acoustic Phonetics*, Chicago: University of Chicago Press.

Latour, Bruno. (1993) *We Have Never Been Modern*, translated by Catherine Porter, Cambridge, Massachusetts: Harvard University Press.

Long, A.A. and Sedley, D.N. eds. (1987) *The Hellenistic Philosophers, Volume 1: Translations of the Principal Sources with Philosophical Commentary*. Cambridge: Cambridge University Press.

Lowe, Sheila. (1999) *The Complete Idiot's Guide to Handwriting Analysis*, New York: Alpha Books.

McNeill, David. (2007) *Gesture and Thought*, Chicago: Chicago University Press.

McNichol, Andrea and Nelson, Jeffrey A. (1994) *Handwriting Analysis: Putting It to Work for You*, New York: McGraw-Hill Professional.

Mendel, Alfred O. (1990) *Personality in Handwriting*, North Hollywood: Newcastle Publishing Co. Inc.

Michon, Jean-Hippolyte. (1872) *Les Mystères De L'écriture; Art De Juger Les Hommes Sur Leurs Autographes*, Paris.

————. (1878) *Méthode Pratique De Graphologie. L'art De Connaître Les Hommes D'après Leur Écriture*, Paris: Payot.

Norwitch, Frank Harley. Norwitch Document Laboratory, http://www.questioneddocuments.com (25 January, 2009)

Rodgers, Vimala. (1993) *Change Your Handwriting, Change Your Life*, Berkeley: Celestial Arts.

Sundberg, J. (1987) *The Science of the Singing Voice*, DeKalb: Northern Illinois University Press.

Index

B

Babylon, xii
'backpack' of emotions, 49
backward flick, 60, 121
backwards lean, 36
balance, xv, 3, 4, 10, 11, 14, 15, 19, 34, 42,
　50, 60, 65, 71, 78, 84, 90, 92, 93, 94, 95,
　108, 117, 121, 122, 127, 137, 139, 148,
　153, 159, 163, 173, 192, 195, 198
Baldi, Camillo, xiv
balloon stem, 55
ballooning loops, 94
baseline, even, 73
basin, 160
being and becoming, 3, 5, 167
betrayal, 60, 62, 82, 84, 116, 125, 143
blame, 34, 37, 49, 127, 172, 173, 196
block printing, 26
bluff, 34, 51
bow-and-arrow 'f', 50, 72, 77, 119, 166
Brady, Bernadette, 4
bridges, 31
brilliance in thinking, 133
Brontë, Charlotte and Branwell, 25
burden, 37, 40, 50, 54, 130, 149, 170, 182
business matters, 142

C

capital letters, 34, 35, 65, 79
capitals
　misplaced, 35
　over-large, 34
　small, 35
cellars, 36, 185
chains, 26, 39, 43, 185
chalice in letter undulations, 30, 89
'change your eyes', 51
charisma, 74
child-like quality, 85
Chinese writing, 46
Chrysippus of Soli, 3
　rolling cylinder of, 3

circles, running round in, 61
'Clark Kent-Superman syndrome', 143
clear boundaries, 49, 83, 90, 97, 110, 173
clear thinking, 19, 21, 63, 108, 131, 184,
　198
Cleopatra loop, 49
clockwise, 44, 45, 46
closed mind, 56, 149, 159
co-creation, xii, 5, 6, 96, 104, 111, 118,
　126, 128, 135, 145, 155, 165
　definition, xiii
Code of Hammurabi, xii
coincidences, 4
colour, xi, xii, 44, 48, 105, 139, 150
combustion - definition, 67
common-sense, 9
compass directions, 20, 42, 45
compliant, 33, 81
computer technology, 24
concealing, 53
concentration, 24, 52, 73, 131, 179
　lack of, 84, 150
confidence, 23, 34, 37, 39, 42, 51, 67, 95,
　99, 103, 106, 112, 117, 130, 131, 150,
　152, 157, 166, 171, 184, 190, 195
　inability to keep, 173, 183
　information held in, 69, 130, 160
　lack of, 21, 48, 52, 63, 148, 149, 179,
　182
Confucius, 12
confusion, 64, 87, 116, 123, 133, 191
conjunction, see aspects
considerate, 14, 30
containers, 36, 37, 38, 47, 48, 63, 93
control, 27, 54, 65, 67, 100, 101, 105, 108,
　122, 130, 142, 152, 174, 182
convention, 27, 35, 74, 83, 111, 149
convoluted flourish, 60
co-operative, 130
counter move, 50
courage, 39, 106
courteous, 14

Other Books by The Wessex Astrologer

The Essentials of Vedic Astrology
Lunar Nodes - Crisis and Redemption
Personal Panchanga and the Five Sources
of Light
Komilla Sutton

Astrolocality Astrology
From Here to There
Martin Davis

The Consultation Chart
Introduction to Medical Astrology
Wanda Sellar

The Betz Placidus Table of Houses
Martha Betz

Astrology and Meditation
Greg Bogart

Patterns of the Past
Karmic Connections
Good Vibrations
Soulmates and why to avoid them
Judy Hall

The Book of World Horoscopes
Nicholas Campion

The Moment of Astrology
Geoffrey Cornelius

Life After Grief - An Astrological Guide to
Dealing with Loss
Darrelyn Gunzburg

The Houses: Temples of the Sky
Deborah Houlding

Through the Looking Glass
The Magic Thread
Richard Idemon

Temperament: Astrology's
Forgotten Key
Dorian Geiseler Greenbaum

Astrology, a place in chaos
Star and Planet Combinations
Bernadette Brady

Astrology and the Causes of War
Jamie Macphail

Flirting with the Zodiac
Kim Farnell

The Gods of Change
Howard Sasportas

Astrological Roots:
The Hellenistic Legacy
Joseph Crane

The Art of Forecasting
using Solar Returns
Anthony Louis

Horary Astrology Re-Examined
Barbara Dunn

Living Lilith - Four Dimensions of the
Cosmic Feminine
M. Kelley Hunter

Your Horoscope in Your Hands
Lorna Green

Primary Directions
Martin Gansten

Classical Medical Astrology
Oscar Hofman

Understanding Karmic Complexes:
Evolutionary Astrology and Regression
Therapy
Patricia L. Walsh

Pluto II
The Soul's Evolution through Relationships
Jeffrey Wolf Green

www.wessexastrologer.com